THE HAMMER OF THE LORD

COLIN MORRIS

THE HAMMER OF THE LORD

Signs of Hope

My word is like a hammer
which breaks rocks in pieces.
Jeremiah 23:29

London EPWORTH PRESS

© *Colin M. Morris 1973*
First published in 1973
by Epworth Press
All rights reserved
No part of this publication
may be produced, stored in a
retrieval system, or
transmitted, in any form or by
any means, electronic, mechanical,
photo-copying, recording or
otherwise, without the prior
permission of the Epworth Press

SBN 7162 0222 0

Enquiries should be addressed to
The Methodist Publishing House
The Book Room
2 Chester House
Pages Lane
Muswell Hill
London N10 1PZ

Printed in Great Britain by
C. Nicholls & Company Ltd
The Philips Park Press, Manchester

THIS BOOK IS FOR

Elizabeth and Kenneth Hulbert

CHRISTIANS — RADIANT WITH HOPE

Contents

Introduction

GOD is not dead – though so far as millions of people in our society are concerned he might just as well be, but that is a different issue. The Era of the theologian mortician has passed, leaving behind a number of books whose value ought not to be underestimated because the prognostications of their authors proved false.

The Church is not dead, though it could be argued that it is mortally sick. It is Hope that has died; not dramatically, not with an audible death-rattle, but imperceptibly as though some malevolent force has slowly but surely turned down the wick of the lamp of Faith.

So this book is about Hope. It is not a contribution to the debate on the Theology of Hope associated with names such as Moltmann, Metz, Bloch, Pannenberg, and a compelling fresh voice from the Third World, the Brazilian, Alves. I am a working parson and not an academic theologian. Until someone publishes a Moron's Guide to the Theology of Hope I am unlikely to benefit greatly from these latest theological developments.

Meanwhile, I have the man and woman in the pew to care for. And it is for them that this book has been written. It started as a sustained argument and then got wildly off course when I discovered that the sources of my own hope are so disparate that I had to approach the theme in the way a lapidary handles a diamond, facet by facet, assessing the stone from a variety of angles.

This, then, is a source-book. Like the street map of a

town, it converges on the Town Hall from boundary points that are all round the compass.

I am not noted for pandering to the complacency of the Church, and it is more than my pride that would be hurt if any reader felt this book was an act of atonement for my former iconoclasm. My basic position has not changed, though my geographical location assuredly has. The Third World from which almost all my earlier books were written has now its own highly articulate spokesmen. They can represent the constituency of the hungry, the exploited and the disadvantaged with a power and authenticity I cannot hope to emulate because I no longer share, even at second-hand, their suffering and anger.

Now I must speak from *amongst* the affluent rather than *to* them. This is not to suggest that the British society in which I now live is without its outcasts – the homeless, discriminated-against, the unemployed. In some ways, the indignities which are the daily lot of the people of the Third World are even more obscene when they are reduplicated at the heart of Western society. Like all Christians, I am called to share the fellowship of *their* suffering and the solidarity of *our* guilt. I can't pretend to be making much of a stab at it, but I shall go on trying. And as I have begun to reorientate myself to British life, it has seemed to me that the death of hope in many areas of the Church is a matter of central importance. For however weak the Church may seem in contrast to its influential past, it can still be a powerful force for injustice and neighbourly love if it is possible to regain a degree of self-confidence that falls short of arrogance but goes further than abject self-pity.

A Church without hope has nothing to offer anyone. It is just a collection of demoralized individuals so concerned about their own survival that they haven't the freedom to offer society the Gospel in its power and comprehensiveness. To many, the Church must have the aspect of a society of cripples offering to teach whole men how to walk.

Only the renewal of hope can liberate Christians from morbid preoccupation with their own fate and make them available for the service of their fellows. The ultimate question of our historical destiny is a matter for God anyway, and we have been driven to putting our hope and trust in him because all other sources of our power have exhausted themselves.

Include Me Out and *Unyoung, Uncoloured, Unpoor* were what might be justly termed demolition books. For that I make no apology. Dynamite has its due function in construction work. But both books evoked the perfectly valid criticism – granted that some if not all of your arguments are sound, what is left to us when you have finished wielding the sledge-hammer? In one sense, this book is my reply to such critics; in another, it most assuredly is not. I have tried to point to sources of Christian hope without pandering to that slick optimism which the hard-headed realist rightly sweeps aside with contempt. He knows the Church's plight *is* parlous, and so do I.

On the other hand, there is little in this book about the political dimension of Christian hope, which is neither an unimportant nor secondary theme. It is a false dichotomy to sever the theological from the political aspects of hope. But the raw truth is that I have not yet thought my way through to a coherent position on what Johannes Metz has called Political Theology. Indeed, I'm not even sure there is such an animal. But my cogitations on this topic have progressed no further than notebooks filled with scribblings Some day, I hope to reduce them to a literary form some self-respecting publisher might be disposed to print.

I can only hope the reader will be prepared to accept this book as a first instalment, incomplete as a thorough-going treatment of its theme but containing some things I think it important to say *now*. He will, I trust, accept my assur-

11

ance that I have not lost sight of the political dimensions of hope. If he's not disposed to do that then I can only stand on my record as a Christian who was, and is, involved in the problems of Statecraft in Africa – a Continent which will allow no one who chooses to share its life to remain a-political.

Like myself, religious professionals are incorrigible pigeon-holers. They like to know whether a Christian writer is of the school of Paul, Apollos, Barth, Tillich or Bonhoeffer. In fact, I am of the school of Reinhold Niebhur whose writings were a lode-star to me in the ferment and turmoil of modern Africa. But I am also of the school of Wesley. Put at its simplest, I believe in a Biblical theology which leads to political radicalism by way of personal conversion. Excluding extreme literalists at one end of the spectrum and raving radicals at the other, it is not difficult to agree a working definition of Biblical theology. It is the other two concepts which need amplification.

By 'personal conversion', I mean a sustained act of will whereby someone chooses to follow the way of Jesus – a decision whose long-term consequence is fundamental character-change. It is the decision to make the priorities of Jesus his own, and to derive the power-source of his life from that which sustained Jesus. I am not thinking in terms of a super-heated pietism which renders the convert unavailable for worldly service. True conversion ought not to waft the convert away on pink clouds of religiosity but transform the pressure-points of his daily life – those concerned with sex, money, ambition, power and a whole welter of disciminatory judgements we make about our fellow-men and women.

And I do not equate 'polical radicalism' with socialism, communism or any other left-wing 'ism'. To put it baldly, I do not believe any Christian ought to be content with our present society. He must engage himself in a crusade to create a more just, compassionate and humane world. It is not my business to dogmatize about which Party political base from which he chooses to operate in order to further such goals. Let him be Conservative, Labour or Liberal. That is up to him, provided he acknowledges he has concluded a solemn covenant with Jesus who not only proclaimed the Kingly rule of God over every area of life but also embodied it. The political radical fights for a good future for Mankind. What position he takes up in the firing line is likely to be more a matter of temperament and background than theology.

That, in brief, is my position. And this book issues from it.

COLIN M. MORRIS

Wesley's Chapel
London, EC1

They invited me to talk to them about Hope. I replied, 'You must be joking!' They weren't joking. They were desperate. Like most reasonable people in our time, they were baffled and bruised, thrashing around in a world made hideous with running sores like Vietnam, Northern Ireland, Bangla Desh and the Middle East; a world swept by powers that seem beyond all human control – demons who dole out caviare and cars to the few and dust-bin pickings to the rest; a world choking on its own detritus and carved up in every conceivable way, Race against Race, ideology against ideology, even Generation against Generation.

There was poetic justice in the fact that they had asked me to speak about Hope at their conference. I had, after all, acquired a modest reputation as a midget Cassandra, a miniscule Jeremiah crying doom, if not from the mountain top then out of the pages of a couple of paper-backs,[1] upon a Church of which I remain a rebellious son and on behalf of an under-privileged world from which I now live in comfortable remoteness. I was hardly the obvious candidate to bring words of good cheer to sadly or wildly dejected spirits – unless with a nice sense of irony they felt that having done more than my share to spread gloom around the place, I ought to be put on my mettle to strike the odd match as well.

When I told a close friend about the invitation, he recited a catalogue of assorted catastrophies culled from the front page of that morning's newspaper, pronounced that it was

15

Mankinds imminent fate to be pounded, polluted or populated out of existence, and concluded that anyone who thought he discerned signs of hope in a world like this was under such mental stress that he urgently needed a long holiday on another planet.

His gloom is widely shared. There was a time when it was the cynic's task to challenge the *status quo*. Now cynics *are* the *status quo* and anyone who dares to raise his voice against the fashionable pessimism of our day is likely to be accused of whistling in the dark to keep his spirits up, or else have quoted at him that dog-eared parody of Kipling's verse: If you can keep your head when all about you are losing theirs – you just don't understand the situation.

Looking back over the past decade, I realized almost with a sense of outrage that though I had thought myself the classical Voice in the Wilderness, I was, in fact, just one more barracker from the football crowd. Indeed, the wilderness these days has become such a seething mass of prophets of doom bawling their funeral wares that the streets of Jerusalem echo hollowly to the footsteps of the odd, unflappable citizen who refuses to be panicked by the wailing beyond the walls. Granted, we cried woe with the sincere intention of shattering complacency but by a process of prophetic over-kill almost succeeded in extinguishing hope as well.

In retrospect, I doubt I would retract more than the odd sentence or two of either of my doleful tracts for the times except where events have overtaken and nullified or vindicated prediction. But having put myself to school again with the genuine 18-carat Prophets, I've learned a thing or two about the paradoxical nature of their craft. Even when they called down God's Judgement upon their society, they had the knack of rounding off their maledictions on a rising note of Promise which pointed their hearers to the pinpoint of light beyond the darkness. So whilst I have no desire to qualify my earlier strictures on either the Church or Western society, I obviously owe a sequel to those who took me seriously; a sort of final chapter that tries to put together the pieces left lying around after my demolition job.

I'm well aware that I find myself in the position of the man who murdered his father and mother and then pleaded for leniency in court on the grounds that he was an orphan. If someone turns out all the lights, he deserves little sympathy if he barks his shins on the furniture. The consistent course might be to buy a white stick; the sensible one is to look around for an alternative source of illumination. And that's what I've done, recognizing, however belatedly, that the Christian may have to give up many things but hope isn't one of them. Ironical though it may seem, worldly despair, which is what I felt about the West observing it from the perspective of my involvement in Africa, is probably a sounder attitude from which to investigate the sources of Christian hope than any secular optimism. Despair can be hope's forerunner; optimism is it's tawdry competitor.

So unless this world is a gigantic lunatic asylum with the inmates running loose – which is a tenable position, though I don't share it – there must be a Gospel of Hope for Mankind as it postures or cowers in the regions beyond hope, awaiting a fate it knows it deserves yet desires to avert.

The Worst of All Possible Times

Few observers of the contemporary scene would quarrel with the complaint of Eliphaz the Temanite in the Book of Job, 'Man is born to trouble as the sparks fly upwards'. That's my story. It is most people's. And one might be forgiven for assuming that we live in the worst of all possible times, though it is necessary to add that men have always believed themselves to be living in the worst of all possible times. Take, for instance, these words:

> *To whom can I speak today?*
> *The gentle man has perished*
> *The violent man has access to everybody.*
>
> *To whom can I speak today?*
> *There are no righteous men,*
> *The earth is surrendered to criminals.*[2]

The author of those lines was no contemporary doom-watcher or Hyde Park end-of-the-world prognosticator. He was, of all things, a civil servant contemplating suicide at the time of Egypt's Middle Kingdom four thousand years ago. Four thousand years later we are still predicting doom for Mankind because there seems no end to violence and the iniquity that smites the land.

Or move on a couple of thousand years. In the Second Century of the Christian era, a great bishop named Polycarp wrote, 'Oh God! What an awful Age you have caused me to live in!' He had a point. He was put to the flames afterwards. Yet that 'awful Age' was the beginning of an unparalleled expansion of Christian influence – which goes to prove that even bishops aren't infallible, nor, alas, incombustible either.

According to the scholar Erasmus, the Sixteenth Century was 'the excrement of the Ages' – though that wasn't the term he used. Yet it was also one of the flood-gates of History through which the Protestant Reformation unleashed new spiritual and political power into the world. We look back on the Eighteenth Century as a period of great political liberation because of the American and French Revolutions. Yet Rousseau, writing at the time, bewailed 'this mess of rottenness within which we live'. And it was an aspirant to the American Presidency, John Randolph of Virginia, who declared, 'This country is ruined beyond redemption'. Sure enough, a few decades later America had to endure the horror and self-mutilation of the Civil War. But

18

out of catastrophe there resulted the abolition of slavery, the booming growth of the most dynamic nation of the West, and arguably the most advanced of all democratic States, built upon a magnificent Constitution which one of America's founding fathers, Alexander Hamilton, in a moment of gloom, referred to as 'this frail and worthless fabric'.

Nor is our own time bereft of cheerful chappies, mostly writers, who make it their vocation to give our morale a much-needed uplift. The avant-garde playwright Ionesco sees little in the world except 'evanescence and brutality, rage and nothingness, or hideous, useless hatred . . . cries suddenly stiffled by silence, shadows engulfed forever in the night'. To Celine, men are 'monkeys with the gift of speech'; to Samuel Beckett, they are 'bloody ignorant apes . . a foul brood'; to Rexroth, 'Life is just a mess, full of tall children, grown stupider'.[3] Even John Osborne's Angry Young Man, Jimmy Porter, from the vantage point of his street stall, concludes that there are 'no fine, brave causes left'.

Who am I to argue with such literary talent? Certainly, there's plenty of evidence around to justify such harsh assessments of human nature. And yet . . . is one utterly mistaken in detecting through this cacophony of stern despair the odd whine of self-pity? Ours is not the first Age to feel the full impact of the irony, tragedy and absurdity of life. But if we pay too much attention to some of our contemporary prophets, we may be the first generation to perish not by the sword or plague or natural catastrophe but to drown in pathos at our unhappy lot.

It is beyond dispute that on every side we are confronted, even deluged, by violence, injustice and oppression which have to be faced and fought. But there's also a remarkable amount of idealism, compassion and toleration being shown in the lives of ordinary folk. So Man must wrestle with a truth and a choice he cannot evade. The truth is that we

19

are always the worst judges of the historical significance and moral fibre of our own time. It is of the nature of all societies to undergo both decay and renewal at the same time. Even as the grass withers and the flower fades, tiny seeds blown by the same wind which has done the damage are hoarding their energy, about to burst into life.

And the choice is strictly theological. In the last resort, we have to make up our minds whether evil is an alien interloper in a good world, or goodness an heroic defiance against the odds in a sad, bad world. We've *got* to make up our minds because as George Macleod and not Confucius said: He who sits upon the modern fence tends to get electrocuted. And it's a *theological* choice because there is ample evidence that Man can sink to depths of infamy or rise to heights of sacrifice and creativity that cannot be explained rationally as natural characteristics of his species.

From our worm's eye view, the titanic struggle between good and evil that rages at every level of life from the human heart to the great collectivisms, may seem to be a battle of equals taking place on unclaimed ground. But it is a Christian contention that every evidence of evil is an act of cosmic defiance, a violation of the moral structure of the universe. We stand, however shakily, for the good, not in a morally neutral world – which would leave all the key questions unanswered, nor in an evil world which spells eventual doom. We stand for the good in a good world, marred, scarred, torn and warped, but still a good world. According to the Book of Deuteronomy, God puts before a discouraged people the choice that confronts them and throws in some good advice – 'I have set before you this day, life and good, death and evil: therefore choose life!' And with breathtaking aplomb, given the morass into which we are sinking, the Christian claims that we *can* choose life and good in the confidence that the universe stands behind us when we do good and resists us when we do ill – 'Why do you kick against the pricks?', God asks a demon-driven Paul. That is an affirmation about the logic of inevitability, a drift of things as inexorable though apparently insignificant as a tiny seedling forcing its way up to the light through layers of concrete.

The Biblical claim that the universe is friendly – biased towards our good intentions – is no cause for facile optimism. In the short run, evil can and does frustrate God's purposes and bring down untold suffering upon men. But it makes a difference to our morale to be able to believe that there is no dark sinister force at the heart of the universe which laughs at our heroism, nor a gaping void into which the goodness and love of which we are capable are poured and lost forever.[4]

Some may be disposed to accept such positive assertions because the Bible makes them, but there are many sceptics who are not so easily convinced or frankly find them incredible or meaningless. Let me, then, call in evidence the most eminent, fluent and humane non-believer of his day, Bertrand Russell. In one of his early books he expressed the conviction that for a man to change the world for the better he must build his life on a 'foundation of unshakeable despair' – which is not as daft as it sounds if you think about it. Yet he opens his three-volume autobiography with a Prologue sub-titled 'What I have lived For'. It begins, 'Three passions, simple and overwhelmingly strong, have governed my life: the longing for love, the search for knowledge, and unbearable pity for the suffering of Mankind', and ends, '... This has been my life. I have found it worth living, and would gladly live it again if the chance were offered me'.[5]

It would be a violation of Russell's integrity as well as insufferable arrogance to claim that he was really a Christian without knowing it, as some theological radicals might be disposed to do when they stumble upon the enigma of a secular saint. But it is fair comment to claim that this great logician, with glorious inconsistency, radiated not despair but hope and infused it into lesser men as he spoke and wrote and suffered for a more humane society. The foundation of his life may indeed have been 'unshakeable despair' – though I doubt many readers of his autobiography would suspect the fact unless they had Russell's own word for it – yet its pinnacle was a firm belief in the power of human creativity and compassion to change things for the better which implies a recognition that the universe is benign – or else why bother to spend one's energy attempting to empty the Pacific Ocean with a thimble?

But curiouser and curiouser. . . . Russell may have rejected the Christian case but he had an acute sense of one of its lynch-pins – the reality of evil. Thus; his Prologue again: 'Echoes of pain reverberate in my heart. Children in famine, victims tortured by oppressors, helpless old people a hated burden to their sons and the whole world of loneliness, poverty and pain make a mockery of what human life should be. I long to alleviate the evil, but I cannot, and I too suffer. . . .'[6]

Now I would as soon put on the gloves and go into the ring in argument against Russell as take on Cassius Clay, but his evident anguish at the ravages of evil surely implies some positive convictions about what stands against and in contrast to it – the good. And not being a philosopher, I do not see how these two powers, good and evil, explain each other. Neither of them can be an Ultimate since more Ultimate than either is the inexplicable fact that they do exist together. They are both parts of a larger 'Something' which contains them.

To strike out still further beyond my depth – those like Bertrand Russell and the *avant-garde* playwrights I have quoted – who seem to give evil a self-consistent, substantive
22

nature as existing in its own right – appear to be saying that the horrid things about human nature they observe and report with regret are only evil because they have made the purely arbitrary choice that it is preferable not to have children starving, old people lonely and victims tortured. But if our appetites for kindness and cruelty have the same moral status why do these prophets of doom not take the easy way out and exhort us to do the same by giving vent to the most bestial and vicious instincts? It is often the writers who take the gloomiest view of human nature who are to be found waving placards in the van of protest movements, crying to a God of Justice in whom they apparently disbelieve to vindicate the oppressed and disadvantaged. Of all contemporary prophets, it was Albert Camus who in his early writings denied God in the name of justice and later began to doubt that the idea of justice made any sense at all without the idea of God.

The truth is that we can avoid making up our minds about such things as good and evil but we cannot avoid making up our lives. And at the level of our every-day behaviour, we do not regard Man's appetites for good and evil as equally valid. We act out our moral judgements – and few men of our century did so with greater integrity than Bertrand Russell. So however inconvenient or embarrassing it may be, the moment someone gives house-room even in the attic of his mind to the possibility that evil, or whatever he chooses to call it, is a potent factor in human affairs, sheer logic forces upon him some order of priorities. Either Evil is the great elemental force which shaped the world and Good its mirror-image, in which case Temple-nudity, the Black Mass and cockerel disembowelling are in order, or else Good is the way things were intended to be and Evil is parasitic upon it, like ivy entwined round a tree or gangrene rotting healthy tissue. But no man outside a padded cell can live with Good and Evil as two realities amongst others,

23

totally unrelated in any way except that they both exist like a Rodin sculpture and a bottle of beer.

Neither a big brain nor a saintly character are essential preconditions for understanding or receiving the Christian Gospel. But a healthy respect for, and even abject fear of Evil, most certainly is. So when clever men talk about our living in the worst of all possible times, I doubt neither their sincerity nor the accuracy of their observation. I am merely intrigued by their assumption that there *could* be better times. Such a conclusion may leave them a thousand miles removed from Jesus' proclamation of the Kingdom of God.

But it's a start.

The Gift of an Open Future

We are living through the death of the stable society where venerable traditions guided action, ancient gods ruled and old men of vast experience occupied by unchallengeable convention all the driving seats. Our diseases no longer respond to that quack's nostrum – The Same Mixture as Before – dispensed as a political programme or economic theory. In sheer self-defence, we have turned our superstitions into sciences, our lode-stones into compasses and our water-diviners' sticks into space probes, to form tools by means of which we can build bridges from the present to the future. We send out in all directions radar beams to warn this Titanic of a world of the icebergs that lie beyond our unaided sight. All to little avail. We still haven't puzzled out how to move onwards and upwards from the worst of all possible times.

Prediction used to be the business of sea-front gypsies gazing into crystal balls in tents decorated with the signs of the zodiac. It is now a respectable science practised by academics with formidable I.Q.s and professorial status, who use all the ironmongery of technology to construct incredibly complex models that purport to demonstrate the interaction of events which have not yet occurred. Marxist philosophers of history operate on the assumption that the future has already happened and need only be appropriated to ensure the withering of the State and the dawning of that bright, new day which heralds the Prolitarian evolution. But the splintering of the Red World and the outrages in Hungary and Czechoslovakia have sapped their morale and undermined their credibility.

Statistics has replaced astrology as the essential tool of the futurologist. Sociologists of religion and theologians of a mathematical turn of mind have latched on to trend-analysis to plot the future fate and course of the Church. Many Methodists, for example, must have flinched when told that membership statistics over the past fifty years had been fed into some university computer which duly pronounced that their Denominational life-expectancy will be little over thirty-six years. The Fathers of the Church scoffed at this intelligence – they could, of course, afford to, since they will be members of the Church Triumphant by then and no one doubts that *its* numbers are steadily rising. Younger Methodist ministers were inclined to treat the figures with greater respect. To put it at its lowest, their pensions if not their faith are at risk if the mechanical monster proves to be right.

But Doctors of Science employed by the Hudson Institute or the Rand Corporation have more faith in the omniscience of computers than the local sweet-shop proprietor who has fumed over the odd computerized gas or telephone bill informing him that he owes 000000.00 pence and unless he pays up he will be taken to court. He might also ponder the intriguing fact that had computers existed in 1872 when horse-drawn transportation was universal, they would certainly have predicted that by 1972 the whole world would be covered seven feet deep in horse manure. But the trend

25

was not merely altered but nullified by the invention of the internal combustion engine – Factor X – which no self-respecting computer could have been expected to take account of without losing its scientific status.

Hence, when computers are employed to predict the future of the Church, the sensible Christian is well-advised to take seriously their predictions but he would also be both foolish and faithless to ignore Factor X – known more prosaically as the Holy Spirit – which, having itself Divine status, is unlikely to accord it to a conglomeration of transistors and printed circuits which don't even look like Jesus let alone talk like him.

In fact, prediction of the future, by whatever means, has little to do with what the Christian means by hope. Nowhere is the Christian promised detailed knowledge about what tomorrow is likely to bring forth. Indeed, if the New Testament is anything to go by, whenever early Christians make predictions about the future – for example, that little matter of the date of the end of the world – they were invariably wrong. The result is that present-day preachers shy like frightened horses from certain New Testament texts and Biblical literalists are forced to tie themselves in knots trying to make the words of Biblical prophecy fit the music of actual events.

Christians possess no apparatus denied to anyone else by which to determine the shape *of* tomorrow. They make a more extraordinary claim, that their understanding of the future comes *from* tomorrow. That horrid word *eschatology* describes a process which is the precise opposite of prediction. It is certainly a series of statements about the End, but with sheer wilfulness insists that the End is not that which comes after everything else – as the cinema-goer or jilted lover might expect. The End is not the culmination of an infinite series of historical chess moves but a way of looking at the present from the perspective of the future, rather like an astronaut getting a novel sight of the Earth from the surface of the Moon. Eschatology magnifies the worm's eye view, or more correctly it is concerned with how we worms can, by a process of conversion rather than evolution, acquire a God's-Eye view of things.

But more of the stereoscopic screen stuff later. For the present we are called to trust God's promise to us of an open future. Things are not irrevocably pre-programmed to grind on to their bleak, black end. Some of the most powerful words in the New Testament occur in the Prologue to John's Gospel – 'To as many as believed on him, he gave them *the power to become. . . .*' The power to become is the promise of an open future, an assurance that we are not frozen, immutably fixed in the present, destined always to be what and who we are. It is this offer of development and freedom which strikes a decisive blow at all stereotypes – insulting classifications of other human beings as Niggers, Yids or Spicks, Limeys, Yanks or Huns. Discrimination against others on the grounds or race, colour, class or sex is not merely sinful; it is plasphemous. The Jews recognized this two and a half thousand years before Dr Geobbels became the deadliest image-maker in history. That Second Commandment – Thou shalt not make unto thyself any graven image – is not just a prohibition against idols; it is a warning that whoever attempts to capture the essence of a person in an image reduces him from a human being to an object. It robs him of his future by abolishing the dimension of the mysterious, the as-yet-unformed aspect of his character

Indeed, on the strength of the New Testament's view of human nature as being in a permanent state of flux – 'Now are we Sons of God and it does not yet appear what we shall be . . .', it is not going too far to state that the future cannot be predicted, except in the most impersonal sense. The future has still to be invented.[7] Tomorrow's Men have still to

27

make their choices, and a risky business it is too. We have the power to become our own executioners or someone else's gaolers; the guardians of their freedom or the dissipators of our own.

In the most personal sense, we invent the future when we face the choices which make up the raw material of tomorrow. We can reject hate and choose for love because it cannot ultimately be resisted; we can stand for truth rather than lies, for as Carlyle wrote, 'No lie can live for ever.' Presumably, the truth can.

Things that Are and Things that Are Not

There is a passage in Paul's First Letter to the Corinthians in which he stands worldly values on their heads and points out how God uses the most unlikely instruments to get his work done. To be pompous about it, we might call this statement Paul's philosophy of history, though if he were pressed to acknowledge the fact he would, no doubt, claim to be much too busy to construct philosophies of *anything* – 'I leave that sort of exercise to the school-men of Gamaliel' he would probably comment over his shoulder as he packed his bags before dashing off to found a new community of Christians.

Nevertheless, there *is* a philosophy of history in these verses which might move us either to hope or despair depending on our track record. 'To shame the wise,' Paul wrote, 'God has chosen what the world counts folly, and to shame what is strong, God has chosen what the world counts weakness. He has chosen things low and contemptible, mere nothings, to overthrow the established order. ...'[8] So far, so good. History furnishes plenty of examples of the foolish, the weak and the despised pitting themselves against the big battalions, and winning. This is the story of freedom movements germinating with five men in a cellar

28

and finally smashing an oppressive system ribbed with steel. It is the story of Kepler who, when his work was banned, shrugged and said that since God had waited thousands of years for an observer of his stars, he, Kepler, could wait a few decades for a reader. This is the story of Spinoza, banished from his home town as a dangerous heretic so that a full century elapsed before anyone dared utter his name. It is the story of Milton getting a meagre £10 for *Paradise Lost* and Mozart being laid to rest in a pauper's grave. Above all, it is the story of Jesus dying an ignominious death and rising resplendent on the third day.

We have no difficulty in accepting such a view of history. But it is Paul's final paradox which seems to defy logic and confound common sense. God, he claimed, has chosen 'things that are not to overthrow the things that are'. That sticks in our gizzard, or at least it ought to, for at first sight it seems little more than a contrary rhetorical flourish.

At least that's what I thought until I was forced to wrestle with this strange business of Hope. Now I think I dimly see what Paul was getting at.

Take one or two mundane examples. A boy chooses and marries the wrong girl and unless he works very hard at his marriage the shadow of the girl he should have chosen will fall across his relationship and finally destroy it. The thing that didn't happen eventually nullifies the thing that did. Or amongst the thousands of daily commuters who pour off the trains at Waterloo Station every morning, there must be those who find every step of the journey to their office desks a martyrdom – stockbrokers who are frustrated doctors, post office clerks who dream of martial glory, typists who would find fulfilment on some mission station in a remote part of the earth – that which never came to pass, for whatever reason, saps the juices of their life and condemns them to the existence of a galley slave. And one might spare a compassionate thought for the spinster who turned her back on a marriage opportunity in order to devote her life to the care of an aged parent. In the eyes of the world she is the epitome of filial affection but deep inside her is a gnawing bitterness. And whenever she plays aunt to someone else's children the thing which never came to pass rises up to choke her.

And isn't every pang of conscience we feel tangible evidence that what we ought to have done, and didn't, still has a terrible power to sour our enjoyment of the fruits of self-indulgence?

All true. But Paul is painting on a larger canvas. The truth he states constitutes a Divine threat or promise over history. Our societies and systems are merely extant alternatives to the creative possibilities still capable of superseding them if they fail to achieve their God-given purposes. Whenever a nation, the Third Reich is a good example, acts from the premise that it has an absolute right to exist at whatever cost to other nations, it invariably destroys itself in the process of trying to prove its indestructibility. It is a terrible pride that blinds us to the truth that any force or power in history which is not of our making has an equal or even greater right to exist than our own.

These 'things that are not' are the invisible pressures of God upon our lives and they warn us that God has inexhaustible initiatives still in reserve. There is one well-polished sermon illustration which I would not only excise from all theological college homiletics courses but also ceremonially unfrock any preacher using it. The story goes that Jesus returns to Heaven and is asked by Gabriel how his earthly expedition fared. Jesus tells the story of his life, including an account of the calling of the Apostles who have been charged to carry on his work. When Gabriel asks what will happen if the Apostles fail to do the job, Jesus replies, 'I have no other plans!'. Fair enough: the urgency of the Christian's task and the confidence God places on him to discharge it is dramatically underlined. But the story is theologically defective and plainly unbiblical. Nowhere in the Bible is it suggested that there might come a point where God will exhaust his initiatives, throw up his hands in impotence and leave the world to its own devices. Even in Old Testament times, when the Chosen People went astray, God took Cyrus, a pagan king, and used him for his own purposes. And somewhere on that homiletical trip to Heaven Jesus must have undergone a drastic change of mind. After all, he once threatened the Jews with the alarming possibility that God could turn stones into sons of Abraham – which hardly suggests a Divinity whose room for manoeuvre has come to an end.

The vast possibilities of creation from 'things that are not' are set as a threat against every existing thing. This is the invisible pressure of God upon history. When we reach the end of our tether, God has still enough rope left with which to haul us out of the pit or hang us. His inexhaustible initiatives are both threat and promise. When Evil seems invulnerable and absolute, those 'things that are not' God can bring into being in order to crush the Powers which claim undisputed ownership of the world.

On the other hand, the hammer of God is poised over the Church which is intended to be the scaffolding of his Kingdom. Should it cease to be an outpost of that Kingdom and become an ertsatz substitute for it, then the 'thing which is not' – the true Kingdom – will destroy the Church and leave us with the taste of dust in our mouths and a handful of ashes in our hands.

So God looms over the future like a hovering hawk or an anxious parent, depending upon the sincerity or otherwise of our intention to stand for his Kingdom. But it would be utter fool-hardiness to trade upon our indispensibility to him. There are finite limits to the number of sons of Abraham around. Stones, however, are plentiful.

One reason for the widespread feeling of hopelessness amongst Christians is their morbid obsession with the state of the Church. Not only do we tend to judge the proximity of the Kingdom of God by our membership statistics – when we flourish, the Kingdom is at hand; when we are in decline, it tarries – but more seriously, we use the Church as a thermometer by which to gauge the state of God's health. To put it crudely, there are sincere denomination-alists who are utterly convinced that should the last Methodist expire God will finally vanish in a puff of pink smoke. Much contemporary talk about Mission is really concerned with something quite different – the survival and revival of the Church. The unspoken question which dominates many of our conferences on Evangelism is not, 'Does he reign – and where?', but, 'How can we win? How do we reverse the Church's downward drift and shake society out of its almost contemptuous disregard of us?'.

I must qualify what might appear to be a serious under-estimate of the importance of the Church's role in the world. Christians dare not sell short the Church because there is a sense in which it is prior to all else in Christianity. Only in the Church is Jesus known and named as the Christ. As John Knox[9] has pointed out, Christian worship is the Church worshipping. The Christian Gospel is the Church proclaiming. Christian theology is the Church thinking. And, of course, the New Testament itself, which is often invoked against the Church, is a product of it. Its authors were not merely speaking *to* the Church but also *out* of it.

All this I freely admit. But I would still claim that the Early Church was preoccupied with a different question from ours. They did not ask '*How* are *we* doing?' but '*What* is *he* doing?'. And if the Kindom of God is the earthly embodiment of Hope, it is unwise to link Hope too closely to the Church's fate. For in the New Testament the relationship between Church and Kingdom is by no means a simple one; indeed, the Bible seems to take a somewhat gloomy view of the Church's prospects, speaking more of humiliation, suffering and death than of glory and vindication.

I also view with great suspicion the evangelical exhortation that we should put the Church's house in order so that we can sally forth to convert the world. I can find little Biblical evidence that renewal, as opposed to Judgement, begins with the Church and then spreads outwards; that it takes place in isolation from and as a prelude to the renewal of the whole Earth. The goal of Mission is nothing less than a New Creation, and the Church's renewal occurs only at the same time and to the same extent as the renewal of the world. Our sole advantage in this process of cosmic manicure is not that we are entitled to go to the head of the queue but that we know the Barber's name, and have more than a suspicion about his method of working.

Yet it is this insistence upon using the Church as the most reliable indicator of God's activity in the world which misleads many Christians into locating Hope exclusively in the past; in a return to some lost and mourned Golden Age. So men of honest evangelical zeal exhort a faithless nation and an apostate Church to 'Get back to God!'. They are asking the impossible – not because the task is too spiritually challenging but because the underlying assumption is theologically defective. Certainly, we could organize a sort of religious Cook's Tour of those places where God once met men, from the vicinity of the Burning Bush, through the Garden of the Tomb and the Damascus Road to Luther's *schlosskirke* at Wittenberg and the plaque in the wall which is all that remains of Wesley's Aldersgate Street rendezvous with God. But it would be little more than an exercise in religious archeology. At any one of those once sacred places

33

we might turn a corner and be confronted, as were Mary of Magdala and Salome on the morning of the Resurrection, with a youth in a white robe announcing 'He is not here. He has gone before you.' There is no way *back* to God. The real problem is almost as daunting, but at least possible. How do we fight our way *forward* to the God who has so far outdistanced us as to be little more than a pillar of smoke on the horizon?

Equally misguided are the Moralists who sigh (or thunder if they have any fight left in them) for a return to the Victorian Sabbath, the Nonconformist Conscience and family prayers. Here my prejudice shows. It's not only that I reject their premise but also fear the glint in the eye of some of them whom, I suspect, pronounce their anathemas upon modern permissiveness out of the same motivation that led Puritans to condemn bear-baiting – not so much because it caused pain to the bear as gave enjoyment to the spectators.

Then there are those Christians who read Church History as a set of biographies of spiritual giants. They tend to snort with disgust at the Church's present leadership and retire to pray for the providential arrival on the scene of a second Luther, Wesley or William Booth so that they may, to misquote Zechariah, take hold of the skirts of one such Mighty Man Re-incarnate, crying. 'We will go with you, for we have heard that God is with you!'.

Some psycho-analysts might interpret such phenomena as the Christian's desire to creep back into the womb. But it is much more fundamental than that and can be traced not to an abberation of his mind but to a scar on his soul. Deep in the heart of Man lives a persistent dream or rather an atavistic memory of a Paradise to whose beauty and security he longs to return. The Myth of the Garden of Eden is no Biblical fairy story. It is a recurrent nightmare of what has been irretrievably lost, like the mourner's image of his beloved – always present in shapes and sounds and smells that elude his senses.

In that profound Biblical account of the way things originally were, Adam, egged on by Eve, did nothing particularly heroic; certainly nothing so Promethean as stealing the fire of the gods. Yet like the man who leaned against a wall and was aghast when the whole building crashed down, Adam set history in motion. 'I did *that*?' he might justifiably protest. What an extraordinary disproportion between cause and effect by any standard! In one hand he clutches an apple core; with a wave of the other he unfolds the saga of history with all its glory and misery; its epic procession of rising and falling civilizations; the discoveries of Science and wonders of Art; the complexities of politics and wars; and the unleashing of those inner personal drives such as sex, ambition and greed, but also sacrifice, creativity and nobility. Adam chose knowledge and therefore freedom. He disqualified himself from the life of Paradise, which is a whole life, innocent of both good and evil; a life experienced without judgement and free from mortality.

But the poor fellow did even more than this. He set Mankind on a one-way journey. There is little point in any of his heirs and successors turning up at the entrance of the Garden, with the largest, rosiest apple the eye of man did ever see, to make restitution. According to a little-noticed detail in the Genesis account, God posted an angel with a flaming sword at the exit of the Garden to bar Mankind's way back. Adam chose knowledge and we must now live with the consequences of that choice. Whatever Paradise there might conceivably be must lie ahead, and only ahead – a Paradise not characterized by innocence of good and evil but gained only by the recurrent choice of one rather than the other, and indeed, the final conquest of the one by the other.

This primeval desire to get back to Paradise is a peculiarly religious phenomenon. One does not meet it, for instance, in Science. The modern astronomer may venerate Ptolemy but when faced with a difficult problem in astrophysics is unlikely to tear up his textbooks and cry 'Back to Ptolemy!'. Indeed, he may well be impatient of knowledge codified a mere 18 years let alone 18 centuries before. And by the same token, Galen was undoubtedly a great doctor – Marcus Aurelius must have thought so to appoint him Court Physician – yet though I am prepared to doff my cap to Galen as one of Medicine's path-finders, I would feel must safer doffing my clothes to my local General Practitioner if I were under the weather. The blazes with leeches! Give me penicillin any day!

That angel with the flaming sword stands as a potent image to keep our faces firmly towards the future. We cannot even rest content with the present. We cannot stake out a plot of ground in the Here and Now and cultivate another Paradise. There is no hiding place from knowledge, which must now be worked through to its ultimate limits. Nor can we renounce the fruits of freedom – ceaseless striving, movement, creativity, destructiveness, tyranny and horror. But there is a more powerful reason why we cannot rest content with the present – because God is not content with it. When Moses asks God what his name is, he gets the opaque reply, 'Call me, "I will do what I will do" '. We know that God is around because things change. He is not content with our present society, and it is sub-Christian utopianism to imagine that he will be any more content with the society we create to replace it.

Yet because God's initiatives were not exhausted when Adam raided the orchard of Paradise, he adds to the bewildering complex moral choices with which history confronts the sons of Adam one further decision which is more momentous than any other. Man can choose to accept or reject God's Christ. Should he say Yes he receives in return no free ticket back to Eden, for not even the Second Adam can get by that Angel with the Flaming Sword. By incarnating himself within history, he binds himself to accept its laws and limitations. But because the track of humanity takes it inevitably through the Easter Garden, those who note the significance of the broken tomb can use their spiritual freedom to follow Jesus to another Paradise, a Kingdom not innocent of evil but built on its ruins. Manning the entrance of this Kingdom is no angel with a flaming sword but a welcoming Father who comes out to meet us with shoes for our feet, a ring for our finger and with the background music of celebration to orchestrate his greeting.

But we must keep our perspectives in line with those of the Bible. The kingdom of God does not come at the end of time; it is coming all the time. Its reality is not separated from me by the length of time which must elapse before the end of time. It is not merely the shape of an eternity beyond the consummation of all things – that is strictly unknowable. The Kingdom is also present in the depth of this moment, which is why, in the only use of the word in the Gospels, the Man on the Cross can turn to the penitent thief and say, 'Today you will be with me in *Paradise*!' The meaning of this enigmatic saying is not exhausted by the assumption that since the thief is dying he is leaving time for eternity. It is Divinely authorized confirmation that in acknowledging the Second Adam, the wretched, glorious man has not annulled but fulfilled the heritage received from the original Adam and so qualified for admission to that Paradise which is neither before nor after history but can be appropriated in the depth of a single moment.

And to be fanciful: is it not appropriate that Jesus promises Paradise to, of all people, a thief, who since he is adept at picking locks and evading the police may be specially qualified to dodge angels with flaming swords? It was after all, a famous Rabbi who, when rebuked for blessing a

37

notorious thief, retorted, 'When the Gates of Heaven are locked tight, it takes an expert to open them!'.

The moral of which is not to suggest that the Kingdom of God is specially suited to those of a burglarious disposition – though I expect there will be a fair sprinkling of them there. The truth is more prosaic. The Angel with the Flaming Sword who bars the way back to the Garden of Eden is a salutary warning to those eaten up with religious nostalgia, who seek the Kingdom of Heaven in a return to a moment or an Age that has gone for ever.

It is an image which reminds us that we must always look towards the future for our hope, but with the important qualification that the future begins the moment after this.

Hungry Men Whose Name is Hope

Fresh light was cast on an almost forgotten experience by a gentleman of no fixed abode who called at the Manse the other day, touched me for a couple of quid, and then having tearfully assured me that the cash would put a few crumbs into the mouths of his starving children, nipped smartly round the corner into the *Lord Nelson* whose front door happens to be visible from my study window. It struck me afterwards that at no point during that embarrassing encounter – I just haven't the knack for doling out charity unselfconsciously – did I ask his name.

That simple omission took me back to the hungry little man who was the hero or victim of *Include Me Out*. I never knew *his* name, either. But here's the odd thing. Although in that book I affirmed in general terms Jesus' identification with the powerless and underfed, nowhere in it did I refer specifically to the one parable in which Jesus spoke of a hungry little man dying at a rich man's door – the story of Dives and Lazarus. Whether it was a genuine oversight or an unconscious desire to avoid Jesus' finger stabbing me in

38

the vitals I'm not now sure. But what I do know is that had I given some thought to that parable I might have prevented some dubious conclusions being made about the incident of the hungry Zambian; not necessarily morals I drew myself but which by default I allowed others to draw.

For instance, there is the theological assumption of the automatic virtue of the poor. Because our consciences are seared by the gulf between our affluence and the shocking poverty of the majority of Mankind, we have a masochistic urge, which I did little in my book to dispel, to assume that poverty is such a cosmic enormity that those who suffer from it are beyond moral judgement; and more, that we rich have had our reward here and now whilst the poor will, of right, inherit a heavenly kingdom where they will enjoy the bliss denied them on earth.

In fact, a closer reading of the Bible shows that every social group has its own distinctive sins. The sins of the affluent may thunder for retribution – greed, complacency, power-hunger and blindness to the claims of justice. Yet there are also the whispering sins of the poor – envy, servility and defensive viciousness – amply excusable in the sense that were we in their condition we should behave fifty times' worse. Nevertheless, crime in the festering slum or over-crowded refugee camp is evidence that even the bearest existence cannot be, by definition, sinless. Of course it is infinitely easier to imagine God exercising his prerogative of mercy in favour of a peasant who is little more than a bag of skin and bones rather than towards the puce-faced, cigar-puffing capitalist in the shiny Rolls Royce. For one thing, luxury limousines are even more difficult than camels to manoeuvre through the eye of a needle. But a whole theology cannot be constructed out of one's emotions, however deeply-felt.

The cup of water given or withheld which is the nub of the Parable of the Sheep and the Goats may have great signifi-

39

cance in determining one's spiritual destiny, but it cannot, of itself, form the basis of a comprehensive doctrine of Salvation. In the Scales of God, social injustice does not equate exactly with utter damnation, though it must exert considerable pressure on the balance. Those critics who quoted Jesus' dictum, 'Man shall not live by bread alone' against the theme of *Include Me Out* did not offer a complete rebuttal of my case since few of them gave any attention to how and why Man lives *without* bread. But they had a point. Presumably even those too weak from hunger to do more than shake or nod their heads must be able to affirm or deny God in the depths of their hearts or else the whole scheme of Redemption founders on a historical contingency – the economic plight of Mankind at a given point in time.

Conceding all this, the Parable of Dives and Lazarus might be viewed as the unwritten final chapter of *Include Me Out*, but not because it offers any solution to the spiritual plight of the hungry in either global or personal terms. Indeed, of all the parables, its meaning seems to me to be the most opaque – except at the most elementary level where it must be assumed that anyone impervious to the plight of the poor with the Bible in his hands and Lazarus at his door is beyond either the sanctions of Hell or the blandishments of Heaven.

We have some small excuse for misunderstanding the parable because of the wide currency given to its popular title '*Dives* and Lazarus'. In fact, the Gospel of Luke makes no mention of the name 'Dives' which, unless my smattering of Latin has deserted me, simply means a 'rich man'. So it is really the story of an anonymous rich man and a beggar who *is* named, granted, his very name – Lazarus – 'He whom God helps' sounds like a somewhat sick joke. If Lazarus is an example of those whom God helps, then God help those he doesn't!

Lazarus has a name. He has little else.[10] It is the only

means of distinguishing him from millions of his kind, ragged, stinking, ulcerous. The rich man has no name because he needs none. His possessions are a means of identification though they don't constitute an identity. He has an address to which accounts may be sent and no doubt a distinctively luxurious means of transportation that draws attention to his every movement. In the daily commerce of living, it is enough. For as any reputable confidence trickster will confirm, you can drive up to a quality store in a Rolls and walk out loaded down with good things on the strength of an indecipherable signature; on the other hand, pitch up on a bicycle and it's likely to be cash on the nail or nothing.

The parable is about what it means to have everything and yet nothing. Heads of State and similar luminaries have splendidly attired attendants, *aides de camp,* whose job it is to anticipate every wish of their masters. Almost before the patrician nose begins to run, they are on hand with a silk handkerchief. That is also the luxury and fate of the very rich. Their every whim is met almost before it has formed itself into a desire. This is surely why Jesus warned the rich they'd have a hard time getting into the Kingdom. Not because they are necessarily nasty human types; on the contrary, many of them are very good people. It is rather that they have been so conditioned to expecting a readily-available cheque-book to open most of the doors in this life, they tend to make the dangerous assumption that even the gates of the Kingdom will swing apart at the flourish of a golden pen. But the Kingdom, from the manward aspect, is a network of personal inter-dependence. And that is a currency of which many of the rich are bankrupt. They genuinely believe that all they require is at hand, and so may never discover their true poverty – not lack of *what* they need but *who* they need. Even their sleep tends to be dreamless because being hard-headed they have no poetic fancies, and what the ordinary man dreams of, they already possess.

So when the rich man dies, Jesus sketches the dimensions of his peculiar anguish in a couple of merciless sentences. He burns with objectless desire. He is a raging torrent of undirected passion. Like a Stone Age man in a modern super-market, he doesn't know what to ask for. His actual request is as pathetic as it is trivial – water to cool his tongue. It would never occur to him to ask for a miracle – release from torment – which might just have been granted to him. For a miracle is an event far beyond one's expectations. And this man has always lived to the limit of his expectations. So the way out into the Kingdom is barred to him. For the Kingdom is for the desperate and the expectant, those who know that nothing short of a miracle will meet their need – not the insipid water of existence but its transformation into rich, red wine; not a finely carved tomb stone to mark their final resting place but the power to raise them from the dead.

Edward Albee wrote a play called *The Zoo Story* which some critics and many of the public described as obscene because its climax is the attempt of a lonely flat-dweller to make love to the caretaker's dog. That is not a theatrical obscenity but a parable of the screaming hell of those who cannot relate to their fellow humans – who through wealth or pride or accident of circumstances have never allowed themselves to feel dependency or know vulnerability.

Which brings us to Lazarus who is utterly vulnerable – to the scorn of the strong, the obliviousness of the rich, even the cruelty of the elements. To lack the will or the strength to brush aside the dogs that lick one's sores is the ultimate in defencelessness. But when he can recruit the energy, Lazarus has the shamelessness of the beggar. He is incurably hopeful, always expectant, totally dependent upon his fellow-men. He has no false pride, cannot affort the luxury of self-respect and will grovel in the dust for a coin or a crust of bread. This is why Lazarus has a name. He is human – humanity *in extremis* no doubt; humanity when its pretensions and posturings have been stripped away. But he is the raw material of the Kingdom because he knows that only a miracle can save him and a daily miracle is necessary for his survival.

So the Parable of Dives and Lazarus is not about Judgement. The description of the fate of each man after death is not a warning of what the greedy rich and the helpless poor can expect when at last they fall into God's hands. Death in the parable is not a narrative device which Jesus uses to draw awesome conclusions about the nature of eternal life. It is not a lens through which we may catch a glimpse of the beyond, but rather a mirror which throws back an image of the Here and Now.

Jean Paul Sartre has said, 'Hell is other people'. That is only half a truth. Heaven, too, is other people. Lazarus' poverty puts him at the mercy of his fellow men, and that is a form of relationship, however degrading. Dives' wealth cuts him off from his fellow-men, so he knows neither Heaven nor Hell; just a limbo of which he is the sole occupant. Even his innate decency is self-defeating. He asks that his brothers may be told of his fate and gets the bleak reply, 'They have Moses and the Prophets'. But if the brothers of Dives share his values the warning would go unheeded. A bank statement, a notarized document, a solid hunk of the walls of limbo – such things might compel attention because they *are* things. But Moses and the Prophets talked about people, about relationships – a foreign language to Dives and his kind. Nor would someone returning from the dead get them to mend their ways. For that would be a miracle, and lives based upon rock-solid facts, the affluent surrounded by all they think they need, neither expect nor desire miracles.

It is probably unnecessary to add that just as this Parable is about revelation rather than judgement, so it must not be invoked to baptize any present economic *status-quo*. Because the grinding poverty of Lazarus makes him a true member of the human race by forcing upon him dependence and vulnerability, this is no argument against engaging in the struggle to transform the earthly lot of the poor and disadvantaged. Quite the contrary. It is a declaration that economic justice is not an end in itself but a means to increasing the number and variety of human contacts; to providing the things needful, and only the things needful, for enriching human relationships.

Though the story of Dives and Lazarus has been described as the harshest of Jesus' parables, it is, in fact, one of the most hopeful. For I am Lazarus and so are you, and we have Jesus' word for it that our vulnerability and dependence places us squarely within the zone of miracles.

Morning, Sun and Moon, and Marching Feet

Is it utter moonshine or cloud-cuckooism to regard the Church as a locus of hope? There is a verse in an obscure Old Testament book to which I return again and again because it describes in the language of poetry four modes of the Church's being which together sketch out the dimensions of a strange hope that lies through and beyond the tragedy of our failure, disobedience and weakness.

The Book is the Song of Songs and the verse runs:

> *Who is she that looks forth as the morning,*
> *Fair as the Moon,*
> *Clear as the Sun,*
> *Terrible as an army with banners?*

I'm dimly aware that the Song of Songs is a labyrinth of critical problems, but I shall, in happy ignorance, proceed to overlook them. For me, this four-fold image of the Church is in no way invalidated by arguments about the authorship of the Song of Songs or the occasion of its writing. It is true *for me* in the same way that the images of Love in Shakespeare's *Sonnets* would be true *for me* even if it were proved that it wasn't William Shakespeare but another man of the same name who wrote them, or even that he wasn't describing Love at all but some other emotion he'd mistaken for it. That, I know, is sheer perversity, but I reckon every man is entitled to a decent ration of it.

Being a phlegmatic Lancashireman, I am always happier with the more 'structural' images of the Church – as Vine, Body or Rock, rather than one as poetic and ethereal as this, but therein lies both its truth and its strength. Christians need constant reminders that God's sparkling wine is always shattering the bottles which contain it: at the sound of his trumpet our laboriously-built walls fall down and we are left with a pile of rubble at our feet. God's ferocity when we try to imprison him, even within our Churches, is terrifying. It was Hosea, the Prophet of Yahweh's Love who had a nightmare experience of God as Marauder:

So now I will be like a panther to them . . .
I will meet them like a she-bear robbed of her cubs
and tear their ribs apart. . . .

In the face of a warning like *that* we dare glory only in the transience of our earthly tabernacles which, when God's Spirit desert them become as unreal as castles in the air or as lifeless as mass graves.

Yet our imagination must be disciplined if we are to translate our visions into programmes. And politics teaches us, if theology doesn't, that all power must be structured, even spiritual power. Hence, the Church can never remain a large number of individuals sleeping in different beds yet sharing the same dream. The time always comes when we

45

are compelled to put four walls and a roof round our more exalted visions. But even in a time of religious pragmatism, when we are, to borrow the theme of an important series of essays, taking soundings rather than drawing charts, we must somehow retain the poetry of the Faith. And that is my greatest count against some of the so-called New Theologians to whom I am genuinely indebted – not that they have robbed us of our faith in the process of outraging the traditionalists. But they have stripped the Christian Faith of its wildly poetic elements. Their prose is so bare as to make *Bradshaw's Railway Guide* read in contrast like *Pilgrim's Progress* and their liturgies are often couched in language too trivial to tell a mundane truth let alone bear the weight of mystery.

So let's strike a blow for the poetic element in Christian hope by considering an unashamedly romantic image of the Church.

The Church 'looks forth to the morning'. The disjunction between darkness and light, night and day, underlines the strangely episodic history of the Church which has known no inevitable progression from weakness to strength, from glory to glory. Her story has been one of sudden ends and strange new beginnings, decay and renewal, humiliation and vindication, death and resurrection. Neither historical forces nor those tides in the affairs of men have finally shaped her destiny. She responds to the pressures of God – sometimes gently impelling, at other times imposing upon her intolerable weight, and occasionally totally removed so that she swells with sheer self-pretension.

The Church waits – and that's by far the hardest thing she's required to do. She waits for the signals of transcendence; for an angel to stir the waters of the pool; for the stone to be rolled away from the sepulchre's mouth; for the Voice that bids her, as it did Lazarus, to come forth. She waits for Morning.

Morning marks the start of an inexorable time-cycle which can be neither diverted nor delayed. The Universe imposes a rhythm upon the life of Man to which he must adapt himself or be caught napping. So by this image, the Church is reminded that her times are not her own; they are in God's hands. Those bursts of Divine power which renew her life are not the results of *our* strategies but of *his* sovereign initiatives. We can say our prayers, plan our programmes, deploy our manpower, but this totality of our busy-ness is mere kindling – dry faggots which rot unless touched by the fire of God.

Renewed enthusiasm and fresh starts belong to morning-time, but so too, does a certain critical revelation. It is in the cold light of dawn that the things of darkness are starkly revealed for what they are. That reference in the Book of Revelation to Jesus as the 'Bright Star of Morning' is not without its undertone of menace, pointing to the time when the game is up for those who love the night. In Man's artificially generated light the shabbiest of garments seems radiant and the most dubious qualities command uncritical admiration. But exposure to the blaze of morning is a time of Judgement.

It is fashionable to talk about the Underground Church and Invisible Christians. And there is good New Testament warrant for the idea of seeds growing secretly and leaven imperceptibly transforming the lump. But our commendable modesty in claiming that this is a time for experimentation rather than dogmatic policies must not blind us to the truth that morning always overtakes our gropings in the dark. Then Underground Churches must suffer a subterranean upheaval and Invisible Christians materialize to be counted.

This is, I believe, such a time. At the price of infinite pain, the Church is being shown the difference between visions and hallucinations, genuine coinage and lead counters. The

47

Lord of the Vineyard has returned from his travels and is auditing the steward's books.

But it is not only the signals of transcendence which stab the Church awake. The discordant noises of the world also

But it is not only the signals of transcendence which stab dent voices. The Church is being shamed or jerked into activity by the Gospel which the world preaches to her in the thunder of bare feet in Africa and Asia, the cry of the prisoner for justice and of the hungry for bread. We know it is morning because the world will not let us sleep on. Was it not Rip Van Winkle who took a sip from a keg of grog in the Catskill Mountains, fell asleep and eventually awoke to find himself a tottering old man and his country independent? Generations of children have laughed at the man who slept through a revolution. Where the world's pain is not waking the Church, its mockery is.

In another simile, the Church is described as 'fair as the Moon'. There is a terrifying stillness about the Moon, a passivity well illustrated by those miraculous television shots of astronauts bouncing like ungainly clowns across its god-forsaken terrain. So far as one can tell, the Moon in itself is of strictly archeological significance – those highly expensive bags of rock samples brought back to earth will at most prove the precise number of billions of years the Man in the Moon is behind the times.

Yet that barren cinder glows with a strange luminosity when the rays of the sun strike it. The Moon is not a primary power-source, a generator; it is a reflector, beaming to Earth light issuing from a source outside itself. So the Moon-image pinpoints a mode of the Church's life which may seem to some unfashionable if not downright reactionary – the necessary passivity of the Church, her gracious ministry of reflectiveness. We need this insight to counter one of our besetting sins, hyperactivity – the neurotic urge to be seen doing *something*. We dash frantically here and there, enlisting ourselves to all manner of causes, sometimes with the result that we only succeed in doing badly what others are already doing well and neglecting things which others are not doing at all.

We quote with approval Dag Hammarskjold's famous dictum, 'In our time the road to holiness passes through the world of action', forgetting that those words were written by a deeply reflective, even withdrawn man. We seem to have come full circle. Once we took refuge in piety to avoid the claims of action; now we are in danger of taking refuge in action from the claims of spirituality. The novelist, William Burroughs, appears to me to be *exactly* wrong when he writes, 'The drama of Western society is this: not having anything to do'. We've plenty to *do*. What we lack is the will to *be*. The Church's problem is one of identity rather than function. Because we do not know who we are, we do not know what to do. We have anaesthetized by frenetic activity that quiet brooding joy and silent anguish which were marks of Christ's ministry of *acceptance*.

We fall short of our calling not because our zeal is fitful but because too much of our thinking is superficial. To use the Pauline analogy of the Body – our muscles are well-exercised; it is our brain cells which are dangerously under-nourished. Not for the first time in our history, we are being out-thought by Marxists, Humanists and the whole gaggle of ideologues who are struggling to make sense of the world and evolve a satisfying philosophy of life. Too much of our apologetic is a pathetic, flimsy thing of scissors and paste – snippets of theological gossip, political intelligence and sermonic anecdotes that are more ingenious than profound. Our attack lacks punch because our main armament is not the Spirit's sword which cuts to the heart of great issues, but the jester's balloon on a stick that pats them fondly on the head.

Do we not stand convicted of having sold short the intellectual case for Christianity? I am not suggesting that the intellectual case is the only case or even the most important one. But possibly because we have been intimidated by the secular Big Brains, we have lost our sense of the grandeur and comprehensiveness of the philosophy of life which is grounded in the Jesus-Event. That intellectual case is in no way weakened because it accepts two necessary limitations on its scope. It observes a proper reticence, a reverent agnosticism, about the strictly mysterious dimension in existence and makes no attempt to explain it away. It also insists that neither Man nor society can, in the last resort, be saved by analysis, however subtle. There is at work in all human situations a deep corruption of the human will which causes many of Man's problems and makes all the others worse. This deep-seated human dilemma demands for its resolution a Gospel of Redemption which issues from the Being of God rather than the cunning application of the human mind.

So odd though it may sound, passivity, the gracious ministry of reflection, is a truly apostolic vocation, a humble turning towards the truth which makes the Church a reflector rather than a generator – beaming upon the world the light of the knowledge of the glory of God in the face of Jesus Christ. Any other illumination the Church provides may be useful but is secondary.

As the Moon symbolizes one mode of the Church's life – *reflectiveness*, so the Sun represents its complement – *passion*. It shows the strength of the Gospel that this clash of opposing qualities has rarely torn the Church apart. Instead, under one banner have marched (though they occasionally got out of step) those who *know* and those who *burn* – mystic and militant, scholar and evangelist, priest and crusader. That unity which is the Spirit's gift has done more than persuade the lion to lie down with the lamb. Any zoo can perform that trick by rendering the lion lamb-like –

50

which is, of course, an act of aggression on the lamb's part. But to make the lion lie down with the lamb and still retain its real ferocity – that's a different matter. Yet the Church has done it – merging cold and heat without producing tepidity; emblazoning on one banner black and white without merging both into pallid grey; joining hot-blooded Latin and reserved Northener; ebullient African and mystic Asian without de-naturing any of them. So Moon and Sun may represent violently opposed modes of being without either negating the other. Both are held together in one galaxy which transcends and effortlessly contains them.

Like the Sun, the Church's passion is meant to generate both heat and light. The Church deals in anger – prophetic, righteous anger at the spoilation of God's Creation and the exploitation of his children. Sometimes our credibility is doubted because we do not appear to feel deeply enough about great human issues. We huff and we puff, we register dissent, we admonish and warn, but there's a civilized moderation, a studied temperateness about our responses which seems a million miles removed from the sometimes incoherent rage of those wild men of the Old Testament. We show that nice sense of balance, pilloried by W. B. Yeats:

> *A levelling, rancorous, rational sort of mind,*
> *That never looked out of the eye of a saint,*
> *Or a drunkard's eye....*

Would to God we might emerge from the desert, wild-eyed, our garments torn, crying aloud for justice for the children of men! Would to God men could read in our eyes that terror which is born of gazing into the mouth of Hell and sensing the enormity of Divine wrath! Would to God our sleep were disturbed by the howls of the damned; that we could taste the sulphur in the air of our time! It is ironic that many contemporary novels and films have as their

51

theme an awareness of the reality of self-constructed Hells; the foreboding of a secular Judgement; a moral urgency which accords well with a Wesley urging his hearers to flee from the wrath to come or a Whitfield conjuring before the eyes of terrified listeners the spectre of the Angel of Death beating his wings about them. We modern Christians tend to dismiss such preaching as garish, primitive, crude. But make no misake, the passion that informed it was genuine. For who but those who know what Hell is like can appreciate the wonder of our salvation? And is there no moral to be drawn from the fact that the crowds pass the doors of churches from whose pulpits sounds the reedy flute of decency in order to pack the cinemas and theatres where strong passion thunders the theme of well-deserved doom?

Passion of such intensity cannot be simulated. It issues from the guts of a man, at a level far deeper than his mind. It is compounded of outrage and fear, and strangely, hope against hope. And it speaks to the case of millions for whom life is torment and death a liberator. This is the backdrop, the scenario against which the Church's encounter with the world is played out. And if we do not share the agony, we forfeit the right to prescribe the cure.

And yet the Sun which can shrivel by its intensity also warms at a touch. Its light can both blind or illuminate. Whenever the Church meets, it is intended to celebrate the true Festival of Light – the bursting in on the world of a radiance which no darkness can quench. When the Republic of Zambia became independent at midnight on October 23rd, 1964, thousands of people gathered together in the streets and on hill-tops to wait out the hours of darkness. Then as the sun rose on the first day of their liberation, the birth of nationhood, they danced and wept, crying 'We are free!'. And by God, so are we free! Beneath all our solemn ceremonial there ought always to be that same immoderate joy threatening to break surface and upset the measured tread of our liturgies. For if the Church does not meet as for-given sinners, reliving the miracle of their liberation, then the *Church* does not meet.

The ultimate paradox is that the light by which the Christian walks issues from the darkness of a tomb. For the Church is the Community of the Third Day. The Resurrec-tion created the Church and it is the inexorable outworkings of the Resurrection which will one day render it void. Theo-logians talk about the eschatological nature of the Church as the Body which lives with the End as a present reality. Well, that's one way of putting it. Another way is to take this Sun-imagery to its logical conclusion. We are told that the Sun is slowly burning itself out. That which can con-sume is itself in the process of being consumed. So, too, the Church will one day be, not consumed, but transcended. That veiling of the Sun's face at Calvary was a portent of the time when those alive with Christ's life will no longer be conditioned by the rising and setting of the Sun, by heat and cold, but by Grace – a new form of power driving through and beyond all natural forces.

But not yet, there's still much battling to do; hence, that final image of the Church as 'an army terrible with banners'. *The* Church, *our* Church – terrible as an army with banners? Somebody's got to be joking! Only a highly developed im-agination could translate the stately gavotte of middle-class feet tripping down the aisle every Sunday into the thunder of a marching regiment. And is any army whose ranks have been so thinned by desertions likely to shake the gates of Hell with its roar of defiance?

Granted all the dismal evidence to the contrary, the Church is precisely this – an army terrible with banners. Nor must the grandeur of this imagery be reserved for those great assemblies of the global Church, impressive in their strength. Every handful of Christians hanging grimly on against impossible odds qualifies for the title ... it's not only applicable to the hundreds of thousands who gather in St. Peter's Square, Rome, or the multi-confessional, many-hued members of the General Assembly of the World Council of Churches. It's also the pathetic baker's dozen saying Evensong in St. Balderdash By The Gas Works and the Primitive Methodists in the High Street competing against a rumbling boiler as they sing 'Lead us, Heavenly Father, lead us' so long as You don't lead us into joining up with the Wesleyans two hundred yards away, let alone the Anglicans in their Norman fortress by the Town Hall.

'For Believers Fighting' was the title of one section of the first Methodist hymn book. And the New Testament confirms that the Christian life *is* warfare, grim and unrelenting. Warfare against whom? Our fathers were in no doubt – against the Devil they would declare robustly. And in the teeth of our faintly pitying smiles and sophisticated theology, they were right. There was even wisdom in their insistence upon giving Evil a personal name to show that there is about it, and always will be so long as time lasts, the subtlety of a malevolent personality rather than the crudity of a blind, irrational force.

Very few people believe in the Devil these days, and everybody at some point or another serves him. 'Believe in the Devil?' the religiously emancipated incredulously ask. But let them take a stroll down the streets of Calcutta or Saigon or Johannesburg or Belfast, or even London at midnight if they dare, and they might just wonder what degree of perverted ingenuity is required to make the world go quite so wrong. To take one simple illustration that might pass for a parable. Somewhere in a university town in the United States there lives a brilliant research chemist. I don't know his name or a single thing about him, but I would make an inspired guess that he is a decent, kindly man, because most people are. It was his technical virtuosity which made possible the addition of an extra ingredient to Napalm
54

so that the burning jelly would stick with greater tenacity to human skin, defying the efforts of its victims or doctors to scrape it off until it had done its disfiguring work.

No doubt, every morning before that brilliant man set off for his laboratory, he would fondly kiss the skin of his children without making any conscious mental connection between that simple fatherly act and the complex chemistry in which he was totally absorbed – otherwise he would have gone stark, staring mad. It makes no sense whatever to call that man sinful, except to the extent we are all sinful. It may be true that at some point he must accept moral responsibility for the uses to which his research are put. Yet the ultimate infamy which produces wards full of children roasting alive in Vietnam issues from an infinite series of decisions taken by fundamentally decent men, any one of whom would cut off his arm rather than do direct violence to a child.

Plain human wickedness is not hard to explain. Any old lag will tell you candidly and without any attempt at self-justification how he got started on what the Sunday newspapers call his Life of Crime. It is the demonic twisting of the actions of good men that is strictly inexplicable in ethical terms. For example, it is sound economics and not crude exploitation that keeps the majority of Mankind below the poverty line. It is devout men – men of Bible and prayer – who are amongst those who roam the streets of Belfast seeking to maim and kill their brothers in Christ. And there are Generals in the Kremlin and the Pentagon who are chess champions, devotees of Beethoven or students of archeology who would unhesitatingly wipe out half the population of the world on receipt of an order from some political Superman, intellectually their inferior and of proven uneven moral judgement.

What can the moralist say in the face of such maniacal nonsense? By what Gospel of self-improvement can such a world be saved? The answer is, of course, that it cannot. Wesley's Fighting Believers knew, like Paul, that they were not fighting against flesh and blood, as though Evil were merely the sum total of human badness. Indeed, the New Testament has little to say about the Fall of Adam and much to say about Principalities and Powers – forces of spiritual darkness which only those who have lived remarkably sheltered lives – avoided news like the plague and foresworn self-analysis – will dismiss as primitive superstition.

For a battle cosmic in scope, the militant Church requires supernatural allies – and it has them in the Church Triumphant. We must not, in assessing our strength against the task ignore those regiments camped over the hill. It may be my advancing age or just possibly the discovery that I inhabit a larger world than I once thought, but I often find it easier to believe in the Church Triumphant than in its Militant counterpart. I fancy the idea of Karl Barth, Paul Tillich and Reinhold Niebhur carrying on their arguments in Heaven, handicapped somewhat by the fact that what they once saw darkly in a glass they now meet face to face, which must render whole volumes of their brilliant speculations irrelevant. It is not only the brain-power of the Church Triumphant which is available to us but also the simple goodness of many in its ranks unknown to all but their kinsfolk and a handful of friends.

So we would do well to wait until the whole army is assembled before we dismiss our numbers as dirisory and our faith weak. 'Therefore, with angels and archangels and with all the company of Heaven. . . .' that constitutes a formidable fighting force, divided in time and gifts, varied in temperament and personal resources but united in a common loyalty to Jesus, by the power of whose Cross the legions of Hell have been put to flight.

Twenty years ago I could not have written in such high-flown terms. The acids of theological scepticism had eaten deeply into my mind and I was a child of a time when only that world was real which could be changed or affected by political striving and hard intellectual activity. Africa, which to the casual observer seems primitive and circumscribed but which has a thought-world infinitely more complex than that of the industrialized West, pushed back my horizons. So my situation is like that of the generation which in its youth assumed the world was flat and had to adjust to the incredible truth that it was almost round.

My theology has suffered a similar sea-change. I still believe as passionately in the importance of the Christian's worldly engagement but my cosmos has expanded to the extent that I am conscious of regions which can only be explored by a willingness to travel inwards, but not alone – in company with that strange army who comprise the Church. Monica Furlong, as always, puts it well:

'The religious man is the one who believes that life is about making some kind of journey; the non-religious man is the one who believes there is no journey to take. ... Apart from the struggles of maturity which form the journey, one might say that there is a kind of pre-journey, and that it is this which childhood, adolescence and young adulthood are about. Ulysses must prove himself on the plains of Troy before the long journey homeward can begin. He must be a man before he can embark upon the adventures of a man. ...'[11]

Undertaking the adventures of a man, that is what the religious life is about. And we march, not as lonely pilgrims, but as part of an army *terrible with banners*. There is, thank God, a healthy anonymity about much Christian service in our day. We no longer find it necessary to wear large labels announcing our allegiance in order to share Christ's ministry alongside men of goodwill. We have recognized

57

that the first priority is to get the job done and then worry about who claims the credit afterwards. But in the ultimate struggle, the Church must, as Paul counsels, 'come out from amongst them', and march openly beneath flying banners. We can afford our service to be anonymous but we dare not allow our Gospel to be muted, not because our pride is at stake but because it is foolish to spike our biggest gun.

I don't need reminding that all this is a view of the Church which many must find far removed from reality. But Christian hope can only be so much beating of the air unless we are sustained by some vision which can set alight our minds, excite our imagination and nerve our faith. This is the Church for which I often weep and at which I sometimes rage and am often tempted to quit. But it is still the guardian of a Gospel without which Mankind will be robbed of hope.

The Small-Scale Individual

Let's scramble down with some relief from the giddy heights of the cathedral spire to street level! Much of the despair of our time stems from the individual's sense of his own insignificance. It's all very well for Arnold Toynbee to attribute the rise of civilizations to the response of nations or tribes to the challenge of difficulty – geographical disadvantage, climatic rigour or hostile neighbours. This may account for the glory that was Greece or Rome, but underlying the theory is an almighty big assumption – that there is some correspondence between the size of the challenge and the resources available to meet it. Any jockey will tell you that there has got to be some relationship between the height of the fences and the length of the horse's legs. It's one thing to ask a world-class athlete to knock a fraction of a second

58

off his time for the ten thousand metres, but only in nursery rhymes are cows expected to jump over the moon.

It is the disproportion between the size of this world's problems and the slenderness of our personal resources for dealing with them that paralyses us and leaves us feeling numb and useless. What Richard Nixon or Mao Tse Tung do may decide the destiny of the world; what our own Prime Minister does can at least affect the price of beef; how the boss behaves can make life pleasant or a veritable hell for his workers. But all our huffings and puffings don't even frighten the dog.

The greatest enemy of hope in our time is the small-scale individual, by which I do not mean the ordinary chap of modest gifts who with thousands of his kind flows like lava through the gates of the massive industrial concern when the hooter blows. God knows what hidden heroism, sacrifice and suffering the little people of the world hide from public view behind a cocky smile, a shrug of the shoulders and a gritted-teeth determination to keep up appearances. *They* are not small-scale individuals but living embodiments of Hemingway's definition of courage – grace under pressure.

Small-scale individuals are those, who whatever their social class or attainments, have stopped believing that anything they think or do changes *anything*. Politicians tend to refer to them condescendingly but, alas, all too accurately, as the 'silent majority'. They are not silent because they are satisfied with the way things are run or because they believe all the political hot-air assuring them that they live in the best of all possible worlds and under the most efficient of all governments. They are silent because they have nothing to say.

The small-scale individual is the end-product of that process of trivializing our society pursued indefatigably by those who control our intake of verbal and visual imagery – from advertising experts to film makers. Never in the history of the world can such a wealth of technological skill and human ingenuity have been dedicated to such paltry ends. Language has thinned out to the point where we shall soon be re-living pre-history and communicating with each other by means of grunts. Non-news is screamed at us daily in headlines of a size which ought decently to be reserved for a warning that the end of the world is at hand. Most baleful of all, though least obvious, is the death of reticence – the writer or artist's search for metaphors which convey deep experiences without destroying the element of mystery in them. Hence, the ascendency of pornography as an art form, which besides insulting our intelligence by allowing sleezy capitalists to make a fortune out of selling us the contents of our own dust bins, also threatens our good taste rather than our morals. For example, the sex act is now universally described so explicitly that it has little more significance than a good belch, and a genuinely mysterious form of communion is reduced to a bout of bedroom acrobatics more productive of sweat than genuine passion.

It is little wonder that the majority have been rendered dumb. When the brain is starved and the imagination stunted, the withering away of the tongue inevitably follows.

For the small-scale individual, life itself has become a spectator-sport. Night after night, with vacant incuriosity, he sits watching the encapsulated images of a world in torment flick across his sight on a 19-inch screen. Night after night, issues that may hold life and death significance for him are reduced to absurdity by the ritual panel discussion where the participants' views are so exquisitely balanced as to ensure utter stalemate, and the contest is strictly timed to protect the public intelligence from exposure to any subject, however important, for more than the prescribed fifteen minutes. To coin someone else's phrase, public affairs has become a matter of the bland leading the bland into every ditch in sight.

Things are in the saddle and ride men. Life is just too much, too difficult and too complicated. *They*, those blessed abstractions – the Government, the Unions, Big Business, the Establishment – *they* will have to sort it all out. After all, that's what we pay them for, or more correctly, what they pay themselves for.

Small-scale individuals are happy captives. They are the ones who preferred to stay behind making bricks in Egyptian labour camps rather than follow Moses on his dangerous journey to freedom. Indeed, they cursed Moses for thrusting a choice upon them. They are of the same breed as the peasants of Southern Italy during the Twenties and Thirties who accepted their lot, whether it was hunger, banditry or facism, as a fact of nature or an act of God. They are Timorous and Mistrust of *Pilgrim's Progress* who when Christian on his trek to the Celestial City meets them and points out that they are going in the wrong direction, reply that the further they go the more danger they meet with; so they have decided to turn back, preferring the fire and brimstone of the City of Destruction to the perils of an unknown way.

That Victorian humourist, Artemus Ward, once wrote, 'I have already sent two cousins to the war, and should the need arise, I stand ready to sacrifice even my mother in law!' – which is another way of putting that parody of Isaiah's words, 'Here am I, Lord! Send someone else!'. The small-scale individual will pass the buck to someone else, to anyone else. Yet it may be that we are unjust in writing him off as a man of straw. Possibly there was a time when he did care deeply enough about something to take a stand for it and was flung aside by the passing of the Juggernaut. The moral he drew was that since he could do nothing to hold up or divert the great impersonal forces which seem to determine human destiny, he will step smartly aside when next he hears those huge, rumbling wheels in the distance. He knows what it feels like to have a toe crushed through trying to use his foot as a brake.

Grant his point. The sources of power in modern society are so diffuse and remote that he is dimly aware of being only a pawn in some war game played by the chess masters of the Kremlin and Pentagon. He's a hole in a computer card, a statistic in the employment–unemployment cycle; a dot on the maps of the planners who trap him between their motorways, fill the space around him with the steel and concrete towers of megopolis and the air above him with noxious gases and screaming jets.

Fair comment. It's all very well castigating the small-scale individual but he could reasonably retort that he feels like that victim in one of Edgar Alan Poe's stories – trapped in a room whose ceiling is slowly but inexorably being lowered on to his head. He sinks to his knees and finally flattens himself like a skin rug, jibbering with terror, until floor and ceiling meet and he ceases to be a man and becomes a layer of meat in a gigantic sandwich. That's a melodramatic way of describing the condition but it does convey the right atmosphere of claustrophobia, the sense of bodily and spiritual constriction which oppresses so many in our time. There is no hypocrisy so outrageous as the indignation of the older generation at the frantic struggles of the young to withstand all the pressures towards conformity. The prison door clanged shut behind *us* long ago. *Their* attempts to mark out and defend some area of freedom and initiative deserve our sympathy if not approval.

There is a morbid fascination in watching the wheel turn full circle again and again as successive generations shape up to the perennial crises of life. The Preacher of *Ecclesiastes* has some claim to the title of Cliché King of the Bible but he was right when he said that there is nothing new under the sun. Each generation nibbles at an indigestible slice of life, and applies novel brands of sticking plaster to the same perpetually bleeding wounds with no noticeable success.

I suppose one sign of approaching age is the wearisome sense of having seen it all before. The controversies which once heated the blood have long since been cooled by the chill winds which blow across old battle-fields. The pendulum swings on. In my student days, the Church winced under the batterings of clever agnostics like C. E. M. Joad who once commented bitingly, 'Hands off the Church of England: it's the one thing that can save us from Christianity!'. Though even that uncharitable judgement was mitigated by the fact that he finally fell into the hands of a country parson and ended his days in the third pew from the front, fervently chanting the *Te Deum*.

All of which is *a propos* of nothing very much except to observe that the spectacle of the less conventional of the young dividing themselves out into revolutionary nihilists and mystical drop-outs takes me back to my first reading of Arthur Koestler's *The Yogi and the Commissar* where the same options as those which face such of our contemporaries as have not stopped thinking, reading and caring, were described in brilliant prose.

The Commissar is a symbol of the logic of revolutionary violence. He believes in a dynamics of history which is irresistible and so co-operates enthusiastically with the inevitable. He would echo Hitler's dictum that history always forgives success, and like a particle of dust in a wash bowl he is carried by the swirling water down the plug hole. The Yogi, on the other hand, doesn't believe in the dynamics of *anything*. He seeks utter detachment from the agonies of existence in a world-renouncing piety. From his mountain peak he observes impassively Life's passing show, refusing to applaud progress or damn regression.

Alas, the choice between Piety and Power is never so clear-cut. Commissars, to their embarrassment, find spirituality extruding from between the cogs of the machine and are forced to adopt an attitude which looks suspiciously like worship towards *something*. The modern Yogi finds utter detachment an illusion because he is drawn, willy nilly, into the relativities of existence. A mountain peak, a bottle of wine and a bowl of fruit may seem tenuous links with modern society. But if the fruit turns out to be South African and the wine Portuguese, he has political decisions thrust upon him – to boycott or not to boycott regimes which deny others the freedom he demands for himself. And anyway, the chances are that his mountain will turn out to be composed of bauxite and sooner or later the bulldozers will growl their way towards him and he will be caught up in the environment argument.

There's a more compelling reason why Yogi and Commissar, drop-out and radical, cannot go their separate ways. They may dream different dreams but they occupy the same bed. There just isn't enough of what the Nazis called *lebensraum* – living-space – to permit the splendid isolation of *Be-ers* from *Doers*. We belong – it's as simple as that. So even the small-scale individual cannot remain content to be one of life's spectators. There is another view of history which orchestrates what the Commissar is saying with what the Yogi is doing but also ensnares the small-scale individual who aspires to be neither. It is a Biblical view which claims that the human dilemma cannot be dealt with by any human resolve but only by Divine rescue. Whether he wills it or not, the smallest-scale of all individuals is playing a star role in a great tragedy, and its essence has never been better expressed than in a single Pauline sentence: 'Oh, sinful man that I am, who will deliver me from the body of this death?'

This, then, is what the Yogi, Commissar and the small-scale individual have in common. Regardless of their personal preferences – to plant bombs under the Houses of Parliament, take courses in transcendental meditation or stay at home and watch *Match of the Day* – they have roughly an equal share in determining the quality of history. And should you feel that a simple affirmation about most things in this life, good and bad, depending upon the character of individuals qualifies as Platitude of the Week, please feel free to post off to me a suitable booby prize. I would stoutly defend that statement as a truism most profound, a superficial truth of limitless depth, a clinché revolutionary enough to set the schools of philosophy in an uproar.

You see, whilst we have been digesting the undoubted truth of Niebhur's arguments in *Moral Man and Immoral Society* that collectivisms such as nations, unions, corporations, etc, are riddled with a sort of structural evil which cannot be explained as the arithmetic sum of the sins of the people who comprise them – and it's taken us forty years to get the point – the small-scale individual has gone gently on his way wreaking havoc. Only the right-down-the-line, Dot-and-Comma Biblical Evangelicals have insisted that all it takes to create a good society is good men. That is not true. But its converse is. Bad men, mediocre men, or those who almost qualify as non-men because of their passivity, have just about wrecked the Joint, to use the idiom of the Western, that modern morality play beloved of the small-scale individual.

History itself provides the necessary evidence. Take just two instances, widely separated in time, but equally instructive. School children are taught that the ancient Greeks condemned Socrates to death. They didn't. 501 men made up the jury which tried him. 281 men voted for his death; 220 voted to acquit him. Had a mere handful of unnamed individuals changed their minds, the course of history might have been altered.

Or this. I knew and had personal dealings with a fitter who was the classical small-scale individual. He was one of thousands who worked in a great aircraft factory, performing endlessly the same monotonous task day in and day out. Then one evening, on the other side of the globe, a giant passenger plane crashed on take-off and all sixty-seven people on board were killed. Board of Trade officials sifted the wreckage for clues to the cause of the crash, an official inquiry was held and by a tortuous process of investigation a link was established between sixty-seven mangled bodies at a North African airport and a pathetic little man in a Midlands council house. A terrible spotlight was brought to bear upon a single worker who, just once in all the thousands of times he did the same old boring thing, made an error which escaped the attention of those whose task it was to inspect his work. And the frightening power of a small-scale individual was convincingly demonstrated, if only negatively.

It's not a point that need be laboured. The small-scale individual can *change* things. He need only take his dog for a walk down the fast lane of the M1 and the resulting carnage will testify to his ability to affect the lives of hundreds of people.

But it's no negative moral I'm trying to draw. Just as darkness implies light and common sense teaches there must be at least two sides to everything – if only an outside and an inside, so a man may be unable to help being built on a small-scale – blame his grandparents for that – but he is still an individual, and at all costs, the tendency to bury this truth under a welter of abstract, collective nouns must be strenuously resisted. As Marshall Foch said, 'It wasn't an army that crossed the Alps; it was Hannibal!'. The military leader is probably more aware than most that you can neither defend a line nor mount a successful attack with a collection of abstract nouns. He knows that it takes only

66

one man to crack and a whole sector may collapse in disarray.

Sir Arthur Keith once claimed that if three hundred individuals were taken out of history we should still be living in the Stone Age.[12] One could justly retort that one need only *add* to history a handful of men of the Hitler breed and Mankind will soon find itself living in a new Stone Age. Granted, Keith was talking of quite extraordinary individuals, but it would falsify our experience to regard all that has been achieved in history as the work of towering talent alone. It was an anonymous engineer-mathematician of genius who designed and superintended the building of the Pyramids, but he'd have had a hard time translating his dream into reality but for the legions of equally anonymous workers and slaves who hauled those huge stones into place.

I would claim that even granted the presence of the towering intellect, the creative spirit, the masterful leader in any age, should courage and hope go out of the lives of ordinary people, nothing could prevent a relapse into barbarism. For the truth is that each of us is more than an individual. We are individuals *plus* the ideas for which we stand. And ordinary men can be possessed by extraordinary ideas, just as a slender wire can carry a powerful current.

The truth of Christianity can be dismissed as illusory and its influence condemned as evil, but what cannot be denied is that the course of history was changed by a few men, not one of whom, with the possible exception of Paul, could have fashioned a novel philosophy or generated the power to captivate whole societies. There is a little noticed detail in Luke's account of the Last Supper. Jesus looks round on his disciples and says, 'You are the ones who have stood by me throughout my difficulties' – a tribute generous to a fault. They had consistently misunderstood his message and mission, quarrelled about questions of status, and were

67

all to desert him when the crunch came. But there was just the merest germ of truth in Jesus' comment. They *had* left their tools and nets and families – ordinary men who had sensed that something extraordinary had invaded their lives – a man worth following, a banner under which to march, a song to sing.

That's how Christianity changed the world – not by all its solemn conclaves, its quarrelling councils and protracted synods, but by an extraordinary idea of a Kingdom for the rag, tag and bob-tail, embodied in the totality of the life of one man, going quietly out into the world and appealing to ordinary people – stand by me! Believe in me!

We talk as though this world is in a mess because we've reached the limit of our ingenuity and run out of ideas by which its tired old life could be renewed. But there's no shortage of world-renewing ideas around. The problem is finding homes for them in the minds and hearts of ordinary people. Justice, world brotherhood, racial harmony, economic opportunity, toleration – these long-term goals don't strike the great world assemblies and national governments like bolts of lightning. They originate from the spot you now occupy. No individual is insignificant who is prepared to stand by, and if necessary suffer for, a significant idea. Take your choice. The field is wide open.

C. S. Lewis, never at a loss for an astringent phrase, was once asked what he would do if he knew that a nuclear bomb had been launched. He replied that in the fraction of a second before the dropping of the bomb and its detonation a man would still have time to say to himself, 'Poo! You're only a bomb. I'm an immortal soul!'. Call such a comment romantic bravado if you choose, but it is the core of a philosophy of life which will allow no one to write himself off as a small-scale individual. Lewis was illustrating a view of history so panoramic that even a world war would be worth a mere footnote, and yet paradoxically, Man the ant, the speck of dust on the planet's surface, must dominate the narrative because God has given him dominion, and even more rashly, organized the universe on a co-partnership basis.

This world is an unfinished work which Man can only make something of as he makes something of himself. Ask for bread and God doesn't drop a loaf in your lap but sprinkles a few seeds in your hands. Demand maturity and God offers only the power of procreation – what you do with the embryo is up to you. Cry for peace and he will grant you the capacity for sacrifice. Yearn for the Promised Land and he will point first to the desert and then to your feet and tell you to get walking!

Even those disposed to acknowledge the truth in such a philosophy of life may be unable to relate the majesty of the vision to the reality of their circumscribed existence. What can possibly restore the dignity of the small-scale individual, eroded away by centuries of acceptance of his role as the plaything of Fortune? Well, take a close look at an incident that occurred about four centuries ago, in the year 1554 to be exact. A brilliant scholar, Muretus, down on his luck, fell ill and was taken to a place where the doctors, deciding that his case was hopeless, proposed to use their ragged, emaciated patient for the purposes of research. Standing by his bed and not knowing who their patient was, one doctor said to another in Latin, 'Let's try some experiments on this vile body!'. Whereupon Muretus replied in faultless Latin, 'Do you call that soul vile for whom Christ was content to die?'.

That's an unanswerable question. Can you call a soul vile for whom *anyone* is prepared to die? Accept for a moment the heart of the Gospel that Jesus died for small-scale individuals – a reasonable assumption since there are more of them than any other human type – then you move into a world whose values are too fantastic to be untrue. Translating the law of the Survival of the Fittest into the moral realm, one might reasonably expect pigmies to die for giants, the mediocre for the outstanding, foot-soldiers for generals, the moron for the genius. But take a good look at Joe Bloggs in cloth cap, boiler suit and boots as he eats his sandwiches and reads the sports page of the daily tabloid. Now ask again Muretus' question, 'Do you call that soul vile for whom Christ was content to die?', and you might get a fresh perspective on a bad, old world.

And if you can get Joe Bloggs to accept the simple truth that Christianity isn't going to inflate him into a Big Brain, a world-shaking personality, but could stiffen his spine, restore or strengthen his self-respect and put into him the stuff of sterling character, then you've uncovered the secret of the early Church's success as an irresistible force for social change. For Joe Bloggs has become an agent of hope, someone prepared to stand by the best he knows in a bad time, in the confident belief that nothing done by an immortal soul can ever, in the last resort, prove insignificant.

What's more, you can with confidence put Joe Bloggs in the ring with the cleverest agnostic of our day, and though Joe can't even spell the word 'agnostic' let alone take a stab at its meaning, he's got the winning punch, for as Dean Inge once said, 'You can confute an argument but you can't confute a character!'.

Neither Utopia nor Armageddon

One looks back with some nostalgia to those halcyon days of yore when only God had the power to end the world. He also has stronger nerves than the jittery, bemedalled custodians of Man's Doomsday machines. These idiot-heroes think it a matter of honour to be just that bit quicker on the trigger than their ideological rivals. To gain for one's own side five extra minutes of existence before the Bang might qualify one for history's final accolade. The snag, of course, is that there wouldn't be anyone around to bestow it.

There must be few outside a mental hospital who doubt that the Hydrogen Bomb is an unspeakably wicked device. Any nation using it to ensure physical survival could do so only at the cost of moral disintegration. P.M.S. Blackett was stating an important yet partial truth when he coined the neat aphorism, 'Once a nation vests its safety in an absolute weapon, it becomes emotionally essential to believe in an absolute enemy'. So America and her Allies in the Fifties waged a Holy War against Communism from the dubious premise that godly materialism is morally superior to godless materialism. It was only in the Sixties that the two Power Blocs awoke to their common predicament – the possibility of Armageddon by accident, the crippling economic burden of the arms race, the importance of winning the support of neutralist nations by bullying, cajolery and bribery, the need to adopt some stance towards the hungry Third World, and so on, and so on. . . .

Yet good and evil play strange tricks in history. The very prospect of nuclear cataclysm intimidated into existence a fragile, grudging world community, living in the shadow of that mushroom cloud. Nations with an honourable history of mutual antagonism heard, as Irish women are said to do, the wail of the banshee at their door, warning that someone, everyone, must die unless all live. Tom Lehrer's tragi-comic lyric, 'We'll all go together when we go!' is a colourful way of stating the more prosaic truth that in the Nuclear Era the whole world is the smallest possible unit of survival.

Such a situation is too unstable to be described as hopeful. The only sensible attitude is one of sober realism which prevents the Christian from oscillating wildly between extremes of optimism and pessimism. Yet the sheer fact of this uneasy amalgam of nations, which is at most a formless

71

organism with a ticking bomb where its heart should be has intoxicated some idealists with a vision of World Government. 'At last Mankind is within reach of true unity!' they cry as they dash to the ends of the earth with their Gospel of Hope. Alas, their hope is illusory, for the nature of hope is the future realization of something that is both good and possible. These visionaries are the noble heretics of internationalism – committed to the proposition that because something is desirable, it must be possible; that *any* historical problem is soluble in our time provided we put more brain power, elbow grease and ingenuity into its resolution.

But it is secular optimism rather than Biblical hope which sees true World Government in the foreseeable future. The stark truth is that history does not offer a single example of nations being prepared to sink their separate identities in a larger whole because they *feared* each other. World community lacks the ethnic, religious, linguistic and historical materials that together provide the cement of the nation – which is, thus far, the highest form of Man's togetherness.

The goal of the advocates of World Government is wholly admirable but in their enthusiasm they ignore a truth which belongs as much to international affairs as engineering – the height of any permanent structure must be proportionate to the strength and elasticity of the materials that compose it. Christian optimists are more eager to chase after noble impossibilities than to wrestle with the ambiguities of what is realistically possible.

Such a sober conclusion doesn't find much favour with keen supporters of the United Nations Organization who regard that massive and elegant skyscraper in New York as the key staging-post on the road to a politically united world. In fact, the U.N. is conclusive evidence of the present impossibility of creating a World Government. It survives only because no member-nation has been required to surrender any substantial degree of sovereignty to it. Paradoxically, it is right of veto that has held the Organization together, which proves that world community has not yet reached that stage of integration where minorities are prepared to trust majorities and great Powers accept any discipline imposed by fellow-members when their national interest is threatened.

God forfend that anyone should take such comments as lack of support for the U.N. On the contrary I am a passionate believer in it, having observed its agencies at work in many parts of the world. It is an admirable body, but light-years away from World Government.

It was the poet, Robert Burns, who wrote that there are some facts which are 'chiels that winna ding' – stubborn truths that are resistant to any pressure and must be taken for what they are. It is a picturesque way of describing the modesty of the Christian hope in international affairs. Assuredly we must move beyond the nation-state, but in carefully measured steps, and testing every foot of the way.

The first stage is the growth of a truly international conscience. Of this, signs appear daily. In an average week, there'll probably be demonstrations in America about British policy towards Rhodesia; protests in London about the treatment of Jews or writers in Russia and riots in a dozen capitals against the Vietnam War. Leaving aside the rights and wrongs of the particular issues, the fact is that more and more people are becoming aware of a responsibility towards their fellow-men in other parts of the world.

Certainly, there are still plenty of Alf Garnets around who believe that the world ends at Dover, and if it doesn't, it ought to; that we British alone made Britain Great and that the proper basis of a foreign policy is to mind our own business and tell everyone else to do the same. Such political troglodytes will probably grudgingly concede that since God unaccountably neglected to endow our island with every single thing needful for existence, we've had to get tied up in foreign trade – but fundamentally we are who we are, self-made, self-entire, and proud of it.

Let's be fanciful for a moment and demonstrate our global inter-dependence by considering the antics of one such mythical Englishman. His day begins as he steps out of his pyjamas – a garment which originated in the East Indies, and he washed with soap invented by the ancient Gauls. He shaves, a masochistic rite first developed by the ancient priests of Sumer and made a little less unpleasant by the use of a razor made of steel, an iron-carbon alloy discovered in Turkestan. Then, down to breakfast. The table cloth is probably made of cotton from Uganda and the cutlery of South African or Rhodesian chrome, nickel from Canada and vanadium from Peru. A cup of Indian tea or Kenyan coffee, a slice of Danish bacon, an egg from poultry whose foodstuffs have been imported from any of thirty countries, ranging from Iceland and Chile to Japan, and he's ready to go.[13]

Alf then dons a close-fitting suit, a form of dress native to the Asiatic steppes; he adjusts his tie, which is, of course, the vestigal remnant of the shoulder shawl of a 7th-century Croat. Then complete with hat which originated in Eastern Asia, and umbrella, invented by the Chinese, he will dash for the train (which, thank God, we British *did* invent). He pauses to buy a newspaper using coins which first made their appearance in ancient Lydia. Then he settles back to scan the day's news – which will be set out in Arabic characters on a Chinese innovation, paper, by means of a German process. He'll snort with disgust at the antics of those dreadful foreigners, and thank a Hebrew God in an Indo-European language that he is 100 per cent – a decimal system invented by the Greeks – English, a word of course derived from Angle, a district in Holstein.[14]

But as Alf would say, we really ought to have been mind-ing our own business all those centuries. He could then have cut a dashing figure in a wolf-skin with a face decorated in woad.

There is no escaping the fact that we are hopelessly indebted to all Mankind for the very sinews of our life. A thousand tiny filaments join us to men of every race under the sun. Nor should realism blind us to the truth that our economic dependence can be divisive as well as binding. To take one instance, the number of children who get some schooling in Zambia is directly related to the copper price in Chile. International cartels, the supra-national corporation, world market-rigging all conspire to keep the poor below the poverty line and consolidate the treasure of the rich nations of the West and Far East. So the interplay of good and evil which punctuates the Bible's view of history operates to weigh down Dives' table with good things and empty Lazarus' begging bowl.

For weal and woe, problems which have become global in scope will demand the gifts and skills of all Mankind for their resolution. The lightning speed at which international aid can be organized when disaster strikes anywhere in the world is a prophetic sign, just the size of a man's hand, pointing to a future when Man's ultimate earthly loyalty will be to his fellow-men. His lesser identities as British, socialist, pacifist, Methodist – to quote a few examples at random – will not be destroyed but fulfilled by the strategies of the one who claimed that he came to do just that – not destroy but fulfil.

Strictly, of course, Man's unconditional loyalty can be given only to God, but it is of his nature to allow Man to grant other men a value which, in dogmatic theological terms, belongs to God alone. God neither dominates the world, robbing us of freedom, nor deserts it, leaving us to our own devices to muddle through as best we can. He inheres within the world in the form of our neighbour – the

75

one whose need we can meet and upon whom we, in return, depend. Thus we can *see* God in the outcast, the victim, the oppressed and even (with greater difficulty) in the rich, the respectable, the well-blessed, because we can *see* him nowhere else. This is surely what it means to talk about the Image of God in Man. Not that we are plastic replicas of an Almighty Being but that there is in us the stuff of divinity, supremely demonstrated historically in Jesus, but discernable in Everyman. We are, as it were, allowed to be humanists by Divine permission.

It is a basic Christian contention that only when Man is prepared to offer unconditional loyalty to God will he be able to burst out of the national, religious and cultural strait-jackets that imprison him and encounter Man as Man. We are not there yet by a long chalk but once our thinking and compassion begins to overleap national frontiers, we have taken a modest step towards a majestic goal. And what is more, we shall be entering the thought-world of the Bible. It is almost three thousand years ago that the Book of Genesis insisted that God made Man, not institutions, civilizations and nations, but Man. And God created and is still creating a world which can only be inherited by Man; not some men, an elite, master-race or Super-Power. No hope is offered in the Bible for men. Only for Man. That is how God arranged things and they will work no other way.

All this is marshy ground, for we skirt the edges of some Religion of Humanity, which would not only be grossly heretical but constitute a sophisticated form of Paganism which has on a number of occasions in history brought its devotees to a disastrous end. Indeed, it is one of the oddities of religious controversy that some critics of Christianity pour scorn in one breath on the doctrine of the Trinity which they usually caricature as belief in a God made up of three Persons, and in the next breath, staunchly affirm their faith in a deity – Mankind – effectively composed of a couple or so billion persons at least.

I am on record as professing that Mankind is my Church,[15] by which I mean that the *ecclesia* or assembly of people that the Bible talks about can never be so exclusive as to baptize only a fraction of humanity and consign the rest to perdition. What Jesus said and did foreshadows an *ecclesia* which must eventually engage all men in the Feast of Life. Mankind is my Church but Mankind is not my God – a distinction it is necessary to keep always in mind when struggling to make world citizenship a reality.

All our heady claims for Man must be interpreted in the light of the Bible's claim that he is the image of God, which in practical terms means that the only adequate perspective upon him is a theological one. You can take Man to pieces in the course of a chemical, biological or psychological investigation into his nature. But it is the job of theology to put all the pieces back together and see him whole, as Man-in-relation-to-God.

The Church's performance may be pathetic and her theology in disarray; nonetheless, her responsibility is awesome. For she is the guardian of Man's wholeness, always prepared to fight off the assaults of those who, for whatever reason, wish to imprison him within some system which takes account only of some dimensions of his being. It is a large claim to make for a weak Church, but she is the last bastion against the unwitting totalitarians or unconscious anarchists who in their possibly sincere desire to exhalt Man for his own sake, paradoxically render him more suitable to be the inmate of a zoo than the inheritor of God's Kingdom.

It is an unpalatable truth that the Church's own history furnishes examples of the very evils she is committed to resisting. Grim Calvinism, power-drunk Roman Catholicism and even flabby liberalism have all done their share

77

to de-nature Man. Let this be penitentially conceded. But the grotesque distortions of the fairground hall of mirrors do not deny the normal proportions of a man. They confirm that he possesses them. The Church must proclaim a truth about Man's future which allows him neither to soar like some Greek God on waxen wings towards an earthly Utopia so that he ends up biting the dust, nor sink into irredeemable despair as he girds himself to perish in some nuclear Armageddon.

The Church has many responsibilities towards Mankind. One of the most important is to see Man whole and see him steadily in order to remind him constantly of his true stature – as a being too small to rule the universe and yet too large to sink back into the animal kingdom.

The Illusions of Optimism and the Ethics of Hope

Christians are, at one and the same time, agents of hope and enemies of optimism. It is utterly beyond me how anyone, Christian or not, can see substantial cause for optimism in this world. In essence, optimism is the brave but erroneous belief that our best efforts must produce proportionately good results. But they don't – and that I needn't bother to prove; history has saved me the trouble. I would certainly affirm the converse: the worst efforts of men can and do make the world even more of a living hell than it would otherwise be. Bitter personal experience, let alone a Biblical understanding of history, gives the lie to any philosophy of secular optimism. A warped world takes our brightest and best intentions and twists them into the material of disappointment and failure. When Paul confessed that he always seemed to be doing the evil he abhorred and yet failed to do the good he desired, he could not be faulted for lack of effort. He had come to know himself as well as the nature of the world he lived in. The Bible makes the stark claim that only from Christ issues light upon which darkness cannot encroach.

There is something essentially morbid about optimism. The optimist's personality is often attractive, but his soul is diseased. It is insensitive to the power of evil. He believes either that evil is illusory – if ignored, it will go away – or that it is a wasting asset like many of the material elements which compose the earth. Like coal or oil, its quantity is finite and will slowly but surely be consumed by the white fire of idealism or humanitarian zeal. Any optimist who has felt the full rigour of evil and survived with an unconquered spirit has disqualified himself from membership of the club. He has ceased to be an optimist and is moving dangerously close to something akin to hope.

Honesty compels me to qualify my argument at this point, but just a little. Many of us know *someone* who is a heaven-blessed innocent, naturally good and joyous of spirit, whose hobby is to stroll through the sinister forests of life, seeking out lions in order to pat them fondly on the head and tigers to pull their tails in fun. Such rare characters not only emerge unscathed but apparently vindicated in their conviction that love given is always returned. They go up to a murderous thug with a smile on their faces and request the use of his razor to sharpen their pencil with. And not infrequently, the villain, to his own bewilderment, obliges. I cannot explain this phenomenon. I merely pause to salute it, and pronounce it a mystery which must not be codified into some philosophy of optimism whose basis is that there is nothing good and bad in this life except what one's own attitude makes so. Being a fervent believer in miracles, I would not contest the evidence of my own eyes were I to observe someone, whether Galilean Carpenter or London stockbroker, walking on water. At the same time, I wouldn't regard what I had seen as a conclusive argument against learning to swim.

Rather more common is that optimism which views the flux of life as a complex version of the law regarding ladies' fashions. Skirts may vary in length from year to year but provided we live long enough, the day is bound to come when dresses consigned to the mothballs can be triumphantly re-produced as examples of *haute couture*. This is the cyclic view of history, beloved of those Christians who regard empty churches as infallible evidence that Revival is on the way. What once was, must again be. Every genuine defeat is a portent of victory. The lower the membership of the Church falls, the more convinced is the optimist that beyond the horizon uncounted legions are marching in the direction of the Church door. The emptier the larder, the faster his taste-buds quiver in anticipation of the feast to come.

It is little short of cruelty to rob the undiscourageably Faithful of their optimism, for they are the Salt of the Earth and the Leaven of the Church. But it must be done, however gently, to remind them that, in the words of a famous Rabbi, God never does the same thing twice. Hence, one must ask those who believe that the past hovers just off-stage, preening itself for an *encore*, when they last met a dinosaur in the local park, felt warm winds in the Arctic, bathed in the glory that was Greece or even glimpsed a map of the world where every continent was a-glow with the proud crimson of British Empire?

Should they be of a classical turn of mind, one might breathe the name of Heraclitus in their ear. He, you may recall, claimed that it was impossible to dip one's toe in the same water twice. No matter how nimble you might be, the current would beat you and sweep *that* bit of water downstream. The only constant, said Heraclitus, is change.

History is unrelenting. It drives on. When men and movements, divided in time, appear identical, one is seeing a mirage rather than a vision. Mr Edward Heath is not a second Albert Schweitzer because he has a penchant for organ music. Mr Harold Wilson could not jot down the Special Theory of Relativity on the back of an envelope on the strength of the fact that he and Einstein shared a common weakness for a pipeful of tobacco. The man next door is not the reincarnation of Ghengis Khan merely because both had Asiatic origins. Such examples are not as trivial as they might seem. Optimists are inveterate caricaturists. Had they been there when Jesus wrote in the sand, the moment he turned his back, they would be constructing a four-volume treatise of systematic theology from his indecipherable marks. Not content to read the Signs of the Times, they will put together a railway timetable of the entire Southern Region from the look on a single porter's face. They count all their geese as swans and are capable of starting a gold rush if they stumble on a dropped coin in a mountain of sludge.

Optimists are apostles of a gospel of progress which the Bible takes great pains to challenge. Is Mankind getting better, growing worse or remaining the same? To the optimist, this is a non-question and he brushes aside all relative or equivocal answers. By definition, Mr Brown of Islington is an immense improvement on what he was ten years ago. Totally unacceptable is the more pedestrian truth that everything depends upon how Mr Brown carries on. He may be both better and worse than he was ten years' earlier – a better father but a worse husband, a keener sportsman but a lazier worker; quicker to take offence, slower to rise to a challenge. And if that is the truth about Mr Brown, then it is an even more daunting task to chart the progress of societies and civilizations. Is present-day Britain, for instance, better or worse than the Britain of fifty years ago? We seem to be a society that treats its children better and its old people worse; in which class divisions have softened and racial attitudes hardened; where more people vote but fewer people make the decisions that really matter; from which the Christian God has been de-throned but other gods are elevated at every street corner.

In the ancient world, men sold themselves as slaves in order to eat, put themselves under the heels of a war lord to protect them from barbarians, entrusted their souls to the witch-doctors to save them from demon-possession. A good case could be made out that they still do. The evils are more subtle and the cures more sophisticated. Scientific progress cannot be denied. Some social progress must be allowed. But the basic human condition is too complex, too subject to profound change at depths that cannot be plumbed, for any easy answers about progress to be credible. Those who confidently profess to know what is best for Mr Brown of Islington or anyone else invariably demand too high a price for their services in making good their claims. The history of this century has been dominated by men holding out one helping hand to their fellows whilst discreetly hiding a club in the other. And when the modern witch-doctors of Politics and Science have finished their work, there is not much evidence that Mr Brown will soon be tucking his newly-acquired angel's wings under the sheets in order to sleep at nights, and still less evidence that he could use them to fly. He would certainly be ill-advised to take a chance and launch himself from the pinnacle of the Temple or the roof of the Shell Building at the behest of the apostles of Optimism.

Nothing makes progress so difficult to define let alone measure as the undeniable truth that by far the most potent factor in human affairs is self-interest. As long ago as 1776 when Wesley was preaching the Gospel of Divine Sacrifice and Universal Love, Adam Smith, the first of the modern economists, was declaring in *The Wealth of Nations*, 'It is not from the benevolence of the butcher, the brewer or the baker that we expect our dinner, but from regard of their own interest. We address ourselves not to their humanity, but to their self-love, and never talk to them of our own necessities, but of their advantage.'

That is an unpalatable truth, but none the less a *truth* with which the optimist cannot come to terms. The sinews of our life are a tangle of endless contradictions – men serve us out of self-interest: Governments imprison us in webs of regulations to safeguard our freedom; through taxation, we get stung in order to enjoy the honey of that hive we call the Welfare State – and so on, and on. . . .

The appropriate image of Mankind's trek through Time is neither that of an arrow speeding upwards nor of a highway thrusting on across country – a tangible link between the origin and destination of our journey. A more accurate simile would be crude to the point of absurdity – and yet true. Mankind is like a drunken wayfarer who has an even chance of falling into a ditch and perishing of pneumonia or finding his way home to a warm bed.

At heart, the optimist, like the pessimist, is a fatalist. What he hopes to be, must be. For him, history has more in common with a diagram than a story. A diagram is neat, logical and complete, so that the end can be seen from the beginning. A story, on the other hand, derives its power from romance and uncertainty. It may end in a lovers' meeting, or in unbearable tragedy; yet again it might peter out or culminate in an almighty bang. Who knows? Even the author may have his doubts. For he will tell you that before he has drafted the first chapter, the characters have taken on a life of their own and begun to dictate the direction of the plot. A true writer sets out to script a comedy and before he has finished the manuscript, it is stained with his tears. As a master of language and narrative, G. K. Chesterton, has pointed out, every story begins with creation and ends with a last judgement.[16]

Christianity is not a philosophy of anything; it is a

story, which by its nature must be told by someone to someone else. And like a story it has surprises, proportions, variations which could not be deduced from mathematical formulae. An ancient genius might work out one of Euclid's propositions without having heard of Euclid. But it is beyond the inventive power of any man to script a story which incorporates the raising of Jesus from the dead without having heard of God. That is altogether too improbable, unscientific, and, in a sense, unfair. Certainly no author who professed optimism as his creed would compromise his self-respect by telling such a story. The Hero might die a sacrificial death, live on in the memory of those who loved him and become a legend to those who had never known him. That is an optimistic scenario, and true to life as well. Yet again, the Hero might overcome the forces which opposed him and either reign in triumph or else return to the obscurity from which he emerged, leaving behind him a secure kingdom and a happy people. That too, is an optimistic scenario which has historical parallels. But Resurrection, Ascension and a Second Coming (to use an unbiblical term which has popular religious currency) are the dramatic metaphors of neither happy nor sad stories. They are strictly inexplicable because they are totally foreign to human experience.

So if history is a story told by someone to someone else and includes a Death, Resurrection, Ascension and Glorious Return, then the someone who tells the story can only be God and the someone to whom the story is told is anyone who has heard the Gospel. In which case, we might do well to abandon the futile task of trying to rationalize, justify or de-mythologize events which are told in God-language. They can only be translated into human thought-forms by means of crude analogies which have as little precision as the yapping of one dog to another about what his Master thinks, feels and does.

I make the point that the Gospel is a *story* rather than a *philosophy* to underline the truth that we cannot be saved by any philosophy, certainly not that of optimism, whose roots are too close to the surface of things to offer a firm stance in a rocking world. But optimism is not merely inadequate; it is downright dangerous, posing a much greater threat than pessimism does to Christian hope. To the pessimist, hope seems impossible; the optimist has more self-confidence – he writes off hope as unnecessary. Hence, whilst the pessimist may be sadly convinced that only a miracle can save him, he is at least dealing in grave matters. The optimist, buoyant and cocky, consigns what he regards as unnecessary to the realm of the trivial. The pessimist, hearing the prison door clang behind him, may still hope against hope for a reprieve. The optimist, in his private Eden, is so captivated by the twittering of silly birds that he doesn't hear the ominous rustling amongst the trees. John Donne wrote: 'I need thy thunder, O God; thy songs will not suffice me!' One is nearer the touchstone of things when trembling at the thunder which heralds the storm, than beguiling oneself with songs which are siren-lures to all but those who can sing them in the aftermath of great striving for God against evil.

So the very possibility of hope depends upon the abandonment of any secular optimism. In particular, we must grapple with that grim truth which I mentioned earlier – in every Age, there are some problems so intractable as to be strictly insoluble. Such problems confound our best efforts not because they are beyond the range of God's sovereignty, but for the more mundane reason that some element essential for their resolution is missing. That missing factor may be knowledge, or lack of adequate machinery to translate visions into reality; it may simply be time – time to allow old wounds to heal and new generations to arise free from the bitterness which divided their fathers.

That such is the way of a hard world offers no excuse for men of goodwill to sit back, fold their arms and bewail their miserable fate. There is a day of small things, just as there is a time of grand strategies. And in the day of small things, men of hope may be reduced to chipping away at a great rock with a feather-duster – realistic in their expectations but undeterred in their persistence.

They can do something else. All intractable situations are two-pronged. There is what might be loosely termed the technical factor, presently beyond Man's control, but almost certainly there will also be a human factor which is potentially within the competence of Man to deal with. Many of Man's most desperate problems lay the world waste not because he hasn't the machinery to cope with them but because he is impotent before the stubborn wills of other men. We have the technical means to deal with the problem of world hunger; it is not beyond the wit or desire of the British Government to evolve a constitutional formula that might create some approximation to social justice in Northern Ireland. But in these cases, as in many others, the technology of survival and the political structures for peace, are nullified by what William Blake, in a vivid phrase, described as 'mind-forged manacles' – the conditioning of history, inbred resistance to change, men's fear of their fellows. History has a way of delivering a swift kick sooner or later to get recalcitrant men off their posteriors and do through dire necessity what they stubbornly resist from choice. Meanwhile, people starve, get blasted and burned, live in terror of their neighbours, make aggressive gestures against their enemies and create general mayhem because those mind-forged manacles retain their iron grip.

The Christian Gospel is free from the illusion that mind-forged manacles will dissolve in the milk of human kindness or can be prized open by the iron bar of regimentation. It sees things whole and sees them steadily and yet still insists that there is a saving possibility in the most desperate situation. This saving possibility is neither a formula nor a promise of supernatural intervention. It is a command to Christians to practise the ethics of hope, which are compounded of patience and expectancy; and further, have a power which cannot be neutralized by the negative reaction of those unwilling to see an old problem in a new light or abandon outworn allegiances or get out of ruts which have the comforting familiarity of a well-worn slipper.

Men can respond to their fellows at any one of three levels. They can obey the law: *do to others as they have done to you*. These are the ethics of retribution, calculated to ensure that nothing changes. This law is reducing Northern Ireland to a society of one-eyed men – the Old Testament injuction – an eye for an eye – being observed with fanatical exactitude. There is a higher law which runs: *do to others as you would like them to do to you*. These are the ethics of optimism – a great step forward, and yet demanding more of unregenerate human nature than can be realistically expected. For it is of the nature of desperate, frightened or hate-filled men to return evil for good. The result is discouragement and often the conversion of optimists into pessimists when they hold out bread and receive only a stone in return.

The third law embodies the essence of the Gospel: *do to others as Christ has done to you*. These are the ethics of hope. They demand from those who practise them a willingness to offer their fellow-men what Christ has offered them – sacrifice, acceptance and renewal through suffering. The ethics of hope derive their power from a transaction in which one can expect everything from Christ but nothing from others. The agents of hope cannot be discouraged for precisely this reason. They make no claims upon their fellow-men and are therefore neither surprised nor disappointed when their initiates are rejected and their love attracts only hatred or indifference in return. Unapologetically, they lay before men Christ's claim upon all humanity, but for themselves, their strategies need be dictated neither by prudence nor the demands of strict justice. For them, nothing is at stake, whether pride or life itself. They are free because Christ has liberated them, and mind-forged manacles are as ineffectual as an empty cross or an unoccupied grave.

Whilst the ethics of retribution and optimism have lamentably predictable consequences, the ethics of hope are open-ended. It is just not possible to predict how men will respond to sacrifice and unconditional service. Agents of hope embody the Grace of God which is poured out regardless of the response it gets. Those who practise the ethics of retribution and optimism are making an investment from which they can reasonably expect some relationship between input and output. Offer other men hatred and you will receive hatred in like measure. Offer other men prudential love and you may get for your pains either kicks or half-pennies in accordance with the law of averages which governs the distribution of good and evil throughout Mankind. Offer men God's Grace and the results are not only unpredictable but irrelevant. Agents of hope are not miracle-workers; just honest brokers, acting as middle-men between God and humanity. They speak their word, do their thing, and then await further instructions from their Principal.

The saving possibility within the most desperate situation is the presence of agents of hope who for much of the time bash away with the proverbial feather-dusters at all-too solid rocks, but when the psychological moment arrives, they abandon their proletarian role and constitute themselves into a body of people prepared to risk all and give all to transform a hopeless situation by providing a hospitable environment for some new initiative.

Louis Pasteur, the discoverer of vaccination, once said that fortune favours the prepared mind. By the same token, the future favours the sacrificial spirit – which is why Jesus commanded his followers to become the leaven of History, transforming it from within not by dramatic upheaval but by countless imperceptible but significant demonstrations of the Grace of God in action.

A *Symbol of Hope – the Clown*

We are constantly told the Church is irrelevant. That is only half a truth. The Church *is* relevant to the life-style of the majority of its members. This life-style, however, bears little relationship to that of society in general. There is no great significance in such a fact in itself. Minorities are not always wrong nor need they conform to patterns of behaviour and values in which they do not believe. The crunch comes when erstwhile Christians, especially young people, find the life-style of other areas of society more vital, colourful and exciting than that of the Church and abandon ship to launch out into a more bracing environment.

There is one obvious factor often overlooked in the exhaustive analyses made by theologians and sociologists seeking to explain the Church's decline. Neither militant atheism nor mature secularity (to use the in-phrase) has decimated the Church's membership. The real cause is much less cerebral though none the less devastating for that. The answer is sheer boredom. Martin Luther King once described Sunday morning – worship time – as the most *segregated* period in the American week. That would probably not be true of Britain, but a good case could be made out for the fact that the period on Sunday between 11 a.m. and 12 a.m. is the most *boring* hour of the week. Round about 11.30 a.m., congregations assume their Sermon-Face – masks of polite attention behind which they engage in an interior dialogue with themselves, the subjects varying

89

from 'What on earth is he going to make of *that* text?' to 'I hope I remembered to lock all the car doors!'.

An assembly of agents of hope may legitimately experience desperation, concern, or even puzzlement during Christian worship. But to spread boredom is the sin for which there shall be no forgiveness. Rare indeed in the average congregation is there an air of genuine expectancy, the anticipation of Good News of a kind that would have sermon-tasters echoing the first words of the frog in the Garden of Eden; 'Lord! How you made me jump!'

Preachers are, as a breed, kindly men, and derive no satisfaction from inflicting gratuitous cruelty upon their congregations. They jazz up the liturgy, setting 'The Old Rugged Cross' to a Beatles' tune, import guitarists, dancers, actors, and as a last resort even guest preachers, to put some pep into the proceedings. Alas, all too frequently, our liturgical acrobatics go just far enough to irritate the traditionalists without coming within miles of the unchurched. We ignore the elementary rule that liturgy is the rhythm of real life, and it just isn't part of the life-style of the average Christian to dance down the aisle with a daffodil behind his ear.

The problem goes deeper. We lack images of Jesus which locate him centrally within the life of our time – images symbolic of hope and therefore of the gladness that lies at the Heart of Things. The images inherited from our godly fathers have lost their power to captivate all but the most traditional Christians. We talk, pray and sing of Jesus as Christ, Messiah and Lord. To most of our contemporaries, a *Lord* is what Donald Soper is – six and a half guineas a day for attending Parliament and wearing ermine on State occasions. *Messiah* is the title of an oratorio by Handel, and *Christ* is either a nasty expletive or the surname of Jesus – Edward *Heath*, David *Frost*, James *Bond*, Jesus *Christ*. Even the name *Jesus* has such accretions of sanctity attached to it that should any Protestant couple announce that they wished to baptize their son 'Jesus', they would be suspected of harbouring grandeur-delusions on his behalf.

One image richly symbolic of hope though at first sight somewhat bizarre impinged on my consciousness in a tantalisingly brief chapter of Harvey Cox's book, *Feast of Fools* – 'Christ as Harlequin'. Months later, the rock-musical *Godspell* blasted its way through Theatre-land, portraying the hero, Jesus, as a clown. Some good Christians were offended by the flippancy if not the outright blasphemy of such an association. In part, their outrage was understandable: clowns of genius are in short supply in modern society so the title has gone by default to red-nosed circus comedians with gargantuan feet who upset buckets of water on each other and trot around the sawdust ring in tiny dogcarts.

The true clown, Charlie Chaplin for instance, projects a richly affirmative life-style that is radiant with both *life* and *style*. In Henry Miller's phrase, the clown is a poet in action. His atttitude to life is richly symbolic of hope; he reacts to his fate, however comical, tragic or absurd it might prove, with sheer grace. His every gesture conveys a good, wholesome truth too subtle and profound to express in words.

Christians ought to explore this image of Jesus as Clown, as the embodiment of a life-style bursting with hope if only because it was the outwardly solemn Paul who urged us to 'become fools for Christ's sake' and could talk of the 'foolishness of God' being wiser than men.

Look again at the Jesus of the Gospels from this unusual angle, and provided we can peel the scales of traditional sanctity from our eyes, we might just catch a glimpse of a life-style upon which agents of hope could model themselves.

Take, for example, the refusal of the clown to conform to the limits of the possible. He *will* insist on riding a bicycle whose wheels are out of kilter or try to walk along a slack tightrope. You don't need to be a Fellow of the Royal Aeronautical Society to predict that he is going to nose-dive into the ground. Sure enough he does. But he picks himself up, dusts himself off and tries again. An occasional refusal to conform to the limits of the possible is eccentricity. To make a habit of it requires flair.

Jesus had flair. Once he was in such a hurry to join his friends who were out fishing in a boat that he forgot it just isn't possible to walk on water. And the universe seemed so stunned at his effrontery that it momentarily suspended the law of gravity. On another occasion, he showed a sublime disregard for the laws of arithmetic and so would not accept the elementary rule which states that five loaves and two fishes into five thousand hungry mouths just won't go! So they did!

I'm well aware that to take such Gospel miracles at face value, even playfully, lays me open to the charge of credulity. So be it. The longer I wrestle with the Gospels the less able I am either to distinguish between history and myth or assign much importance to the difference. The Gospels record the total impact of an extraordinary personality upon the community that gathered round him. And at this distance in time, trying to separate out what happened from what they thought happened seems to me to be an utter waste of time. The scholars go on about what actually occurred, how Jesus really ticked, why the Gospels were written and what hidden motivations impelled their authors. I distrust such backward projections, not because I am a New Testament scholar – of that, not even my worst enemy could accuse me. But I am, allowing for due modesty, an author. I've had the odd book given the hatchet treatment by critics – about that I have no complaint; it's an occupational hazard of the writer. But I do marvel at the critic's apparent ability to read my mind and ferret out the secret motives that caused me to put certain thoughts on paper. In one case, an American professor assured those who read his review of *Unyoung, Uncoloured, Unpoor* that a particular passage conclusively demonstrated that I was a guilt-ridden sybarite (that threw me – I didn't know whether it was something one ate, suffered from or practised secretly behind closed doors). I do know, however, that the chunk of biting prose he singled out owed more to a violent attack of indigestion that the unbearable pangs of conscience.

With every respect for the godly learning of Dr Rudolf Bultmann, I happen to believe that the Gospel stands more in need of *re*-mythologizing than *de*-mythologizing. As a scholar I am not fit to tie Dr Bultmann's shoe laces, but I do know one thing about him. He never wrote a Gospel. Certainly he has written numerous important works about the New Testament to which I am indebted for a thousand insights, or at least nine hundred and ninety-nine. The odd insight is lacking not because Dr Bultmann is deficient in scholarship, but because he isn't old as Methusalah. He wasn't there when the man Jesus made his sledge-hammer impact upon a group of men in one place, who had then the task of trying to put their thoughts and experiences into some kind of orderly record. The trouble is that the only men who could challenge New Testament scholars like Dr Bultmann are dead and so cannot argue. But they knew what they knew. They were stunned, bewildered, marvelling witnesses of what Jesus actually said and did.

So I shall stick firmly to my belief that when the Gospel writers described a miracle it was because something extraordinary impinged upon their senses. And the fact that many scholars have ruled that miracles just do not occur doesn't impress me overmuch. All they are saying is that the methods of scholarship cannot be applied to what, by definition, defies rational explanation. They couldn't taste that water in Cana of Galilee and rule out any flavour of wine, nor put their finger on the pulse of Lazarus and pronounce him medically dead. The miraculous is outside their field, but this doesn't prove that it never happens.

My vote goes to the view that historical fact provides the nouns of the Gospel story, and mythology the adjectives, but only a combination of the two forms a complete sentence. If a gospel writer tells me that the same man he broke bread with also stilled a storm then I believe him. For I'm not sure it isn't a greater miracle that one filled with the stuff of divinity should share one's dinner than be able to juggle around a little with climatic conditions.

What the Church celebrates as the Resurrection is the supreme example of Jesus' refusal to accept the limits of the possible. He would not allow even the ultimate biological law to separate him from his friends. And if you retort that it's insanity not to conform to the limits of the possible, I'd have to agree, though I would wish to add that had it not been for those throughout history who have refused to accept such limits, we should still be living in caves, our minds darkened by fear and superstition, at the mercy of the elements. And what is true of progress in the physical world must also apply to the world of the spirit, which is, after all, the same world seen from a God's-Eye point of view. How can we know what Man is capable of until someone thumbs his nose at the stern realists and jumps over the wall?

The clown dares to live out his dreams, whatever the personal cost. And such men are dangerous. They introduce a wild, unpredictable element into an otherwise tidy, soulless, prudential existence. This clown, Jesus, set up his Kingdom in a tiny backwater of a great Empire and declared a handful of peasants to be pathfinders of a new humanity. He talked and practised absurdities about loving one's enemies, cherishing the unlovable and unlovely, and claimed that forgiving and being forgiven are the most sublime human achievements. He established a fools' paradise, a colony of

94

clowns – men and women who dared to live out their dreams, and pay whatever price was asked of them for the privilege.

There are two kinds of people who refuse to conform to the limits of the possible – madmen and clowns. Both may end up behind prison bars, in strait-jackets or on crosses. But sometimes they display such inspired foolishness that they change the world by the sheer power of hope, transforming today's impossible ideals into tomorrow's practical realities.

Or consider another feature of the life-style of the clown – his role as an affectionate social critic. Recall if you can three of Charlie Chaplin's famous films, each of which made a great social evil its target – *City Lights* attacked the soullessness of modern urban life; *Modern Times* challenged the mindlessness of endlessly repetitive labour; and *The Great Dictator* exposed the heartlessness of totalitarianism. Chaplin's social criticism was no less effective because it was completely free from hatred. Indeed, he managed to convey something akin to affection for the essential humanity of those whose policies he roundly condemned.

This is the clown in action as a social critic. His weapon is humour. His strategy is to disarm his enemies by getting them to laugh at themselves in the act of laughing at him. He strikes without wounding and criticizes without rancour, and because he is utterly without bitterness he does not add to the tidal wave of hatred which every evil sets up.

Here we touch the raw nerve of one of the Christian's most perplexing dilemmas. He is both called to speak out boldly against an evil and still love those who perpetuate it. I happen to think that many aspects of South African society are an affront to justice and human dignity. But if at the same time as I voice my condemnation I also give the impression of detesting every white South African, then my criticism may be just but it cannot be Christian. To damn a system and *hate* those who uphold it may have the virtue of consistency but it is not an option open to a follower of Jesus.

What, then, can I do? I could do worse than study the strategy of Jesus who, like all true clowns, was an affectionate social critic. There is a rich vein of comedy running through the Gospels. But it is comedy with a serious purpose. Confronted by any evil, Jesus' method of attack was not that of portentous pronouncement or pious condemnation. Instead, he usually used the weapon of irony.[17] In a sharp sentence, a graphic word-picture, a short parable, he cuts to the heart of the evil, exposing not only its moral enormity but also its inherent absurdity. And this he does without diminishing the essential humanity of those whom he is attacking. His humour was pointed but not wounding. Only rarely did he descend to sarcasm, and invariably his targets were the religious people of his day.

To do this sort of thing requires hardly-won skills – imagination, sensitivity and, above all, compassionate understanding of the frailties which drive men to do evil. The point of Jesus' wit was not to humiliate but redeem. He invited men to see their actions in a different moral context. He was uncompromising in his resistance to evil, but the rigour of his judgement was tempered by an awareness that the most wicked of men is still a child of God and sharer in a common humanity unless he uses his freedom of will to contract out.

The strategy of laughter is man's last protection against the idolatory of all forms of earthly power. Laughter is hope's final weapon. I once read a first-hand account by an Austrian psychiatrist of his experiences in a Nazi extermination camp. He described how the wretched inmates passed beyond terror to the point where every morning when the commandant appeared with the dreaded list in his hand of those chosen for the gas chambers, the victims found themselves laughing out loud at the portentousness of the daily ritual. This extraordinary phenomenon was not caused by hysteria. Laughter, he suggested, was the one way in which the prisoners could assert their essential humanity in brutalizing conditions. For who, in the last resort, has the greater power – the one who has life and death control over others or those who can laugh at the one who has life and death control over them?

Voltaire once prayed: 'O Lord, make my enemies ridiculous!' The clown prefers to use the weapon of laughter in an attempt to disarm and soften his enemies rather than burn or batter them into submission. Laughter is a key ingredient in any strategy of hope. It is the clown's essential armament. It was also Jesus' most commonly employed method of prophetic denunciation.

Another characteristic of the clown is that he is a vulnerable lover. There's a ritual ending to almost every one of Charlie Chaplin's films, where the Sweet Young Thing who has befriended him and shared his misadventures rushes towards him with her arms outspread. Charlie amazed and delighted, steps blushingly forward, only to find it's the good looking bloke standing next to him whom the girl embraces. Charlie winces a little, then shrugs, adjusts his bowler at a jaunty angle and ambles off whistling into the sunset. And the closing music is drowned by the sound of hundreds of cinema-goers loudly blowing their noses.

Charlie never gets the girl. But his unwillingness to learn from bitter experience is only exceeded by his incurable expectancy. When the next film opens, there he goes again, galloping off splay-footed after another hopeless love. It is the clown's fate to be a vulnerable lover. Because his heart is bursting with kindness towards his fellow-men, there's no room in his head for the thought that anyone might bear him ill-will in return. Not once, but dozens of times in each plot, Charlie goes up to a bully with a smile on his face and

97

his hand outstretched – only to be punched on the nose for his trouble. But he keeps on trying, finding endless excuses for those who cause him pain.

The clown's working philosophy is that the universe is benign, people are basically good and that love will take the chill off the coldest heart. And he's got the bruises to prove it! He's a cheerful, walking punch-bag for anyone who cares to work off their aggression or animosity on him. Some might call him a mug, but it is, in fact, a kind of deadly innocence – the beguiling power of the hopeful.

If the decision to choose for love in a world such as this is strictly the act of a clown, then Jesus was the biggest fool in history. He matched love against power, love against authority, love against disease, love against malevolence. Sheer madness! Lack of discrimination in his choice of friends, innocence of political guile, contempt for worldly prudence, openness to the claims anyone might make upon him – such foolishness breaks every rule in society's book, and so rendered his end inevitable.

The Gospels describe a classical Clown's Progress. Men begin by laughing with him, then at him, then their laughter turns to mockery, then they suspect he is mocking them and their sneers escalate to hatred and finally they rid themselves of the disturber of their peace. One of the earliest Christian paintings depicts Jesus as a crucified figure on which is the head of an ass. Experts have long argued about the symbolism. Possibly the simplest explanation is best – if someone is so assinine as to live by love in a hard world he will come to a sticky end.

Sure enough, Jesus *did* come to a sticky end. But with the true clown's resilience, he bounced back into history and was soon at his old game again – wearing down the stubborn wills of men with his unflagging concern; refusing to accept that human character is immutably fixed at the level of its lowest instincts. He didn't always win. He still doesn't always win. How could he, given the fact of free will? But occasionally the miracle happens – life calls out to life and by some mystical chemistry I do not pretend to understand a withered spirit blossoms, a long-locked door opens, and love entices out into the light someone whom all the coercion in the world could not move.

And so another clown is born – and the world, though it may not understand it, has been enriched by a new source of hope.

One final note. It is impossible to ignore the clown's celebration of life. Why is it that we laugh at the antics of Charlie Chaplin with a catch in our throats? Why has every great clown the power to move us to laughter one moment and tears the next? Is it not because comedy and tragedy spring from the same root? Both have their source in our sense of incongruity between what life is and what we know it could and should be. And Man alone of all creation experiences comedy and tragedy because he alone is aware that despite his arrogance and power he is at the mercy of ridiculous or ghastly happenings outside his control.

Westerners segregate comedy and tragedy into clearly defined pigeon-holes. Many of the so-called primitive peoples do not accept this arbitrary division. They experience life as a unitary whole, through which tragedy and comedy are closely interwoven. I once witnessed the funeral of a chief in the Zambesi Valley, and I was first appalled and then intrigued by the air of festivity about the whole ceremony. Everything was noise and smoke and feverish activity. The chief's cattle had been slaughtered to provide a great feast for a hungry people, and his wives were quite literally dancing on his grave; and this, not because they were glad to be rid of him for by all accounts he was a humane and much respected man.

The tribe were celebrating a significant event in their lives, just as they celebrated with equal abandon harvest and drought, birth and death, parting and reunion. In the teeth of tragedy they were affirming life and hope. Such peoples do not ignore or attempt to belittle the dark side of life. How could they, since hunger, disease and violence are their constant companions? But because they accept the sheer *givenness* of life, they are able to transmute these grim realities into the usable coinage of living.

It's easier said than done, as anyone who has known great tragedy will testify. But it is the genius of the clown that he can do it. He unites in himself all those experiences of life which our society has fragmented. Take one of the great clowns of modern fiction, Zorba the Greek. When the slide on which he has worked so hard was destroyed, he doesn't react by wringing his hands and wailing. Instead, he performs a fierce dance that expresses defiance of disaster and affirms the worthwhileness of life – not just the happy bits, but all of it. That dance was a great cry of 'Yes!' drowning out all the negations which belong to despair.

Jesus the clown had this ability to celebrate life. Like a jester he defied custom and scorned authority. Like a wandering troubador, he had no place to lay his head, and like a minstrel he frequented parties and dinners, upsetting the guest-list and bringing with him his disreputable companions to outrage the social conformists. He gathered together a motley army of outcasts, peasants and rogues, and marched at their head to take a great city in a parody of martial conquest.

And wherever he touched life, he transformed it, turning tragedy into victory and misery into joy. He shared the secret of his Kingdom with anyone who cared to ask – a Kingdom at present hidden in the mundane business of living but one day to be made manifest in a great Feast from which no one need be excluded. He tumbled his way through life, affirming that the universe is friendly because God is Fatherly; that life is good and Eternity still better. Like quick-silver, he eluded the grasp of those who tried to put him in his place, and when they finally nailed him down, before they had turned their backs his Spirit was bursting out all over the place. And so in the saga of the Clown of Nazareth, the last laugh was on Pilate and the power-hungry, Caiaphas and the stern moralists, and upon death and the grave.

Ironic though it may seem, I doubt that the world will ever take Christians seriously again until they are prepared to become fools for Christ's sake. And that poses a painful question for people like myself, passably respectable, reasonably prudential, settling inevitably into a behaviour pattern dictated by the mores of my profession and the damped-down fires of middle-age. The whole life-style of Jesus challenges our society and the Church, and also challenges me personally. Have I any right to hope unless I can loosen up and *live*?

A Brief Note on a Big Subject – Babel to Pentecost

It is of the nature of Man to create tangible symbols of his achievements. He plants his national flag on the Moon and signals his intention of further conquest in the pointing finger of the space-probe that hurtles past the moon like an express train through a way-side station. He creates imposing structures to house and advertise his massive organizations and often puts up statues to the men of power who built them. And because Man's achievements are breathtaking, his hopes are limitless. His *credo* is that if Man wants to do *anything* badly enough, sooner or later he will invent or discover the means to do it.

But out of the murky past there looms a myth which if he is wise will give him pause. The story of the Tower of Babel at first sight seems to embody a truth which belongs to the primitive stages of religion – the idea of a jealous

101

God. In fact there is subtlety about the Myth which Man, no matter how sophisticated his thinking, would be foolhardy to ignore. The God who destroys the Tower of Babel is pronouncing judgement on the refusal of Man to accept his finiteness. The moral of Babel is three-fold, and simple. Man is mortal – that is his fate: Man refuses to accept the limits of his mortality – that is his sin: Man's proudest achievements are reduced to dust and ashes – that is his punishment.

Every civilization is, in the eyes of God, a Tower of Babel. Man's restless mind and adventurous spirit tempt him not only to annihilate physical space and bridge every gap in human knowledge but also to abolish the distance between himself and God – to occupy, as it were, Heaven, by refusing to curb his ambition and accept his allotted role in Creation. Man's gravest sins are by-products of his greatest achievements and not his most bestial acts – which is why Babel takes the form of a tower and not a trench.

Because Man is mortal, it is his historical destiny to be cut down to size whenever he develops the symptoms of giantism. As Reinhold Niebhur has pointed out,[18] Man's most impressive monuments to his own greatness invariably become memorials to the death of the achievements he hoped to celebrate. The Egyptian pyramids were barely completed before the civilization they symbolized had decayed and perished. The Justinian Code was the epitome of the grandeur of Roman Law, but by the time it had been expressed in final form, the Roman Empire was in ruins. Thomas Aquinas was probably the last man in history who knew everything there was to be known, yet what we now call his medieval synthesis was cracking within a century of his death and by the 16th century had split wide apart.

Or move into the 20th century. Is it mere coincidence that the tallest man-made structure in the world, the Empire State Building, was completed in the same year that the

Great Depression devastated the American economy with the result that many floors remained unoccupied for years? Is there any moral to be drawn from the fact that the paint was hardly dry on the League of Nations' Building in Geneva before the rape of Abyssinia by Mussolini shattered the illusion of World Community being brought into being by Charter and Edict? Ought one to see any connection between the rise of the World Council of Churches and the decline of organized Christianity?

One by one the Towers of Babel crash to the ground when prodded by God's finger. Their foundations may be solid; it is their pinnacles that are unstable because they are constructed of earthly materials unable to withstand the force of the winds of Heaven.

So according to the Myth of Babel men are punished for their arrogant pride by being scattered across the face of the earth, unable to communicate with each other. The crashing of the Tower is the beginning of cacophony – meaningless sounds that produce only noises devoid of harmony or relationship. It would be silly to attempt to anchor the Myth in history. Man never has had a universal language, if we ignore the pre-verbal gurgles of infants. But what the Myth is implying is that when men had a common centre to their lives, the things which bound them together were more important than the things which divided them. Men addressing God have only one language – that of worship – and that is a mode of communication which overleaps linguistic barriers. When Man ceases to address God and seeks to *become* God then he enters into a state of multi-centred existence, competing for the allegiance of his fellows.

The Myth of Babel describes a human condition redolent of confusion and totally without hope. And were it to stand alone in the Bible without a counter-part, then Man could only bow his head, acknowledge the truth of it, and abandon himself to whatever fate overtook him for the sin of claiming finality for his achievements. But there are no loose ends in the Bible – God always finishes his sentences though his words may seem intolerably far apart. There *is* a counterpart to Babel – Pentecost. Men gather together in one place, are filled with the Spirit and rediscover a universal language. And as the New English Bible puts it:

'... at this sound a crowd gathered, all bewildered because each heard his own language spoken. They were amazed and in their astonishment exclaimed "Why, are all Galileans, are they not, these men who are speaking? How is it then that we hear them, each of us in his own native language? Parthians, Medes, Elamites; inhabitants of Mesopotamia, of Judaea and Cappadocia, of Pontius and Asia, of Phrygia and Pamphylia, of Egypt and the districts of Libya around Cyrene; visitors from Rome, both Jews and proselytes, Cretans and Arabs, we hear them telling in their own tongues the great things God has done." And they asked, "What can this mean?" '

What, indeed, could it mean? The curse of Babel has been cancelled. Men are once again brothers because they are joined together in Christ who died and rose for all. Many, the majority, do not know, but that does not alter the situation. Jesus has become a centre around which all men can cohere, reconciled in their conflicts and transformed from competitors into comrades. The infinite distance between God and Man, which Babel could not bridge, has not merely been spanned. It has been abolished by, in and through Jesus.

In the language of religious orthodoxy, the Spirit is the gift of the risen Christ to the Church. Hence, the Ascension, or more strictly, the Ascendancy of Christ is the declaration that the End of humanity is not dissolution but glory; that Manhood has been taken up into God. But this is the work of God, not the multifarious labours of men on their precarious scaffoldings, tinkering away at Towers destined to crash to earth when altitude becomes more important than attitude.

And the Spirit's gift is a common language – not a sort of religious *Esperanto* – but the language of united worship and common service. A Christian elite has been formed, not from the spiritual superior or the morally elevated, but from those who have heard and appropriated the word of judgement and grace which God has spoken in Jesus. This elite is the creative minority which embodies hope because it sees already what others cannot see and acts on behalf of all humanity. The elite will not always, in worldly terms, prevail, but it will change history.

So the babble of Babel is countered by the language of intercession. Some men, possibly a mere handful, address God not only on behalf of all *his* People but on behalf of *all* people. And the original euphony of Creation is restored, and not just for the odd hour or so. Somewhere on the face of the Globe, someone will be speaking for humanity in the language of prayer every moment of day and night.

From Babel to Pentecost is a long, long journey – over 1100 pages in my Bible. Yet it can be accomplished in the twinkling of an eye – the time it takes a man to see that no work of his head or hands or heart can bridge the gulf which separates God from Man, Heaven from Earth. That realization is not enough. Indeed, it may serve only to deepen our sense of hopelessness unless we take a closer look and recognize that this awful gulf is an optical illusion. It no longer exists because Jesus has not merely spanned but closed it once and for all. And there's a certain aptness in the image of the horny-handed workman of Nazareth as a filler-in of trenches rather than builder of bridges, or an erector of towers.

If this is true, then the world is no longer the sphere of the

105

exclusively human, but a glorious admixture of the Heavenly and the Earthly, with the odd whiff of sulphur in the air to remind us that Hell too has its place. So Man has cause for hope. Despair is not merely inappropriate but downright indecent in a world shot through with the reconciling power of God.

Third-Hand Jewish Wisdom

Attending a Conference recently in the United States, I got into conversation with a young professional theologian presently engaged in completing his master-work – a Ph.D on a Christian heresy so obscure that I couldn't even pronounce its name let alone understand why they burned at the stake the poor chap who thought it up. But when I mentioned *my* master-work for which the only roasting I'm likely to suffer is at the hands of the critics, he produced a voluminous note-book which appeared to contain summaries of all the lectures he had heard at every conference he had attended since attaining the age of puberty. One set of notes was made at a symposium held in 1968 to commemorate the centennial year of the University of California. The particular lecture had been given by a distinguished Jewish philosopher, Professor Emil Fackenheim and its subject was 'The Commandment to Hope'.

The title excited me. There has been no shortage of books by Old Testament scholars on the Messianic Hope. To have the perspective of a contemporary Jewish scholar on this theme was bound to be of great value. There was, however, a snag. The young theologian was obviously destined for great things because his handwriting was virtually illegible, and to get the gist of Professor Fackenheim's thought was like trying to decipher the Dead Sea Scholls. Perhaps the learned Rabbi has published his lecture by now; if so I have been unable to trace it. So the most I can offer you is third-hand Jewish wisdom, fervently hoping that I shall not be sued for plagiarism or misrepresentation. Where I came across gaps in the argument or abandoned phrases so enigmatic as to tax the skill of a professional code-breaker, I inserted a zircon of my own into the bracelet of pure diamonds, for like all the best Jewish scholarship the argument had a limpid quality compounded of simplicity and profundity. In what follows, the wisdom belongs to Professor Fackenheim: I hold the copyright on any confusions or perversions of truth unknown to any Jewish rabbi living or dead.

Professor Fackenheim quotes a rabbi in the Talmud who wondered what sort of questions he might be asked at the Last Judgement. Some were obvious and concerned honesty in business, strict observance of the Torah and the search for wisdom. One question however was startling because it appeared to embody a contradiction – 'Have you hoped for the Messiah?'. How can anyone be *commanded* to hope, any more than they can be instructed to love or ordered to have faith? Yet this paradox has haunted Jewish history and is as near to an explanation as one is likely to get for the extraordinary fact that the Jewish people have survived at all, kingless, homeless, defenceless, bound together by nothing more substantial than a dream.

The Covenant which the God of all men made with one particular tribe was to have deadly consequences for them. He transformed them from an ethnic group into a living parable of hope against impossible odds. And as Jeremiah discovered, God would not allow them to cry, 'Enough is enough! The Deal is off!' The Covenant was unbreakable. Disobedience brought down punishment upon them but no abrogation of the strange bargain God struck with Abraham. And how some of those Jews must have cursed the old Patriarch! The passing of the years seemed to bring no nearer the Messianic Age when men would beat their swords

107

into ploughshares and sit under their vines and fig trees, knowing fear no more.

How vitally necessary was the commandment to hope is revealed in the stories of Jewish wisdom which are a picturesque but depressing record of the frustration of the Jews' natural expectations. Let two examples stand for the rest. One day, two Rabbis walked through the gates of Rome, around which were congregated legions of beggars. One beggar proved to be the Messiah. The rabbis asked him the Supreme Question, 'When will you come?' He replied, 'Today . . .'. They waited no longer but dashed home to prepare a great feast. He did not come, so the following day they returned to the gate and querulously demanded, 'What did you mean by not coming?'. Whereupon the Messiah replied, 'You didn't hear me out. I had only quoted the first word of a sentence from Psalms – "*Today* if you will hear my voice . . ." '. This is a recurrent theme in Jewish writings. If men would obey the Law for a single hour or observe in all particulars one Sabbath, the Messiah would come.

Or again, here is an Hasidic story. A rabbi moved to Palestine to be right on the spot in case the Messiah should come during his life-time. And sure enough, on a certain day, the good man heard the sound of a trumpet from the Mount of Olives, which is the traditional signal for the arrival of the Messiah. What he didn't know was that the trumpet had been blown by a prankster playing a practical joke. The rabbi rushed to his window to look upon a redeemed world only to see in the street a driver beating his donkey. He sighed and said, 'That's enough for me. So long as people still beat their donkeys, the world cannot be redeemed'.

So the Jews lived through frustration and disappointment. God had to *command* them to hope, for how else could they survive conquest, dispersion, discrimination?

Yet all the terrible things which befell them in Biblical times and throughout the centuries of the Christian Era were only a preparation for their ultimate time of testing, described by Dr Fackenheim as The Holocaust.

If any event in recent history might justly be described as the Holocaust it was the use of nuclear weapons against Japan. But for the Jews, the Holocaust occurred at Oswiecim, the county town of the Cracow Province of Poland. You may be forgiven for finding that name unfamiliar. Its other name was Auschwitz – 15 square miles of extermination camps where, between 1940 and 1944, over 4 million people, mostly Jews, together with some Poles, perished. For the Jew, Auschwitz rather than Hiroshima is known as The Holocaust, not because it was their own people who suffered mass obliteration rather than the Japanese, but because there is a rational explanation for the dropping of the Atom Bomb on Hiroshima and Nagasaki. Some military strategists argue that the Bomb shortened the War and so saved hundreds of thousands of lives. It isn't an argument I personally find convincing, but it has a certain logic about it. But Auschwitz, on the other hand, is symbolic of the utterly demonic. It was the encompassing of evil for evil's sake, and that alone. Indeed, in military terms, Auschwitz was counter-productive – Eichmann diverted trains needed to carry supplies to the various battle fronts in order to transport Jews to the death camps.

The non-Jew cannot begin to understand the scar which Auschwitz left upon the Jewish psyche. Over a million children died at Auschwitz not because of their faith nor in spite of their faith. They paid the price for the faith of their great-grandparents, who refused to abandon their Jewishness and assimilate with the European peoples amongst whom they lived. Indeed, the terrifying irony is that had 19-century German Jews abandoned their separate identity, it is possible that some of those who were gassed at Auschwitz might well have been Nazi executioners rather than Jewish victims.

After Auschwitz, it is an extraordinary act of faith for any parent to bring up his child a Jew. For what guarantee can there be that somewhere, at some future time, the unspeakable may not occur – that any Jew may be condemning his great-grand-children to a more sophisticated re-enactment of the same horror?

Amongst Christians at the present time, the Theology of Hope is all the rage. But much of the theoretical argumentation is like the squabbling of children compared to the mind-searing agony of post-Auschwitz Jewry. Which Jew has not asked himself: Was God at Auschwitz? Dr Fackenheim's reply is to quote the testimony of Elie Wiesel, who found himself at the age of 14 transported to the death camp, and by a miracle survived. Wiesel describes an incident in which thousands of inmates were assembled to watch the ceremonial hanging of a small boy for the crime of stealing a crust of bread. As he watched the victim twitching on the end of a rope, Wiesel muttered, 'Where is God now?' The man standing next to him whispered, 'He's hanging upon that gallows'. We Christians who 'Survey the wondrous Cross' before we go home to a good Sunday lunch would do well to keep reverent silence in the face of such enormities. As Honorary Jews, having made an act of voluntary identification with Jesus of Nazareth, we have been granted the privilege without the pain of knowing what it means to be part of God's Elect.

This is the basis of the commandment to hope – *survival*, sheer survival. So thousands of Jews rebelled in the Warsaw ghettos and hundreds died in order that one Jew might escape. Why? In order to tell the tale of the suffering of his fellows. For had the Jews been obliterated without trace then Hitler and his like would have won a posthumous

110

victory. *A* Jew, *any* Jew, had to survive, to make the suffering and death of millions of the rest worthwhile.

The whole question of the conversion of Jews to the Christian Faith is a snake's nest of historical and theological complications. On this matter I stand where Reinhold Niebhur stood – a position which brought down upon his head a weight of opprobrium which would have broken a lesser man. Christianity and Judaism, maintained Niebhur, are two religions with one centre, and it is the role of Christianity to carry the prophetic message to the Gentile world. And whether the Jews choose to share our Christian experience, it is our privilege to share theirs.

So the commandment to hope is the imperative to survive. Just that. Christian hope derives strength and power from the unbelievable resistance of the Jews to all attempts to obliterate them from the face of the earth and in so doing render null and void their majestic testimony to the one God who is the only possible focus of the unity of all mankind.

Christians would do well to learn the moral of those enormous piles of Jewish bodies, frozen in anguish, bulldozed into mass graves like fossilized branches of long-dead trees. The commandment to hope is the Divine insistence that believers must survive, in ones or twos, in dozens or hundreds, so that no pantheon of unholy gods, nationalistic, ideological and materialistic, can demand the allegiance of men and transform a basically good world into a howling bedlam of competing, demonic powers.

One might justifiably claim that the odds against Christian belief in the modern world are overwhelming. But when the Christian is tempted to despair he would be well advised to remember that every Jew born since Auschwitz is the embodiment of an act of faith beyond his comprehension. For would we not baptize our own children into *any* faith which might avoid their exposure to that degree of

111

malevolence which the Star of David attracted, and could attract again.

Put at its simplest, the Christian's first duty is to survive *as a Christian*. God bless Johannes Metz, Jurgen Moltmann, Ernst Bloch, Frederik Polak, Ernst Kasemann and their like who are plotting the dimensions of a Theology of Hope, Christian or Marxist. But they are thinking and speaking in an upper stratosphere of ideas too complex for the average parson, let alone the regular pew-dweller, to understand. Yet the commandment to hope as a Divine insistence upon religious survival is well within the mental range of Joe Bloggs who occupies a seat in his local church, chapel or tabernacle and is often tempted to throw in the towel because money gets tighter, numbers fewer, and buildings crumble about his head. For Joe Bloggs, sparingly talented and bemused by all the novel theological ideas that bombard his ears, shares the dignity and sacrifice of his Jewish brethren who walked or were carried into the gas chambers rather than deny the God of Abraham, Isaac, Jacob and Jesus. He is an Honorary Jew, and many of God's best friends were Jews. Their history is his history. They kept the faith, and so long as a single human voice, in whatever language or accent is native to it, sings the *Te Deum* or recites the Creed, hope will not vanish from the earth.

Dr Fackenheim ends his lecture by pointing out that the living skeletons who staggered out of Auschwitz after its liberation by Allied troops gathered in groups to recite the Kaddish – the Jewish prayer for the Dead. It is an odd prayer because it never mentions the dead; instead, it gives glory to God, returning to him his sceptre and crown wrenched from him by the bereaved in their grief and despair. And those inmates who still had the power of rational thought must have wondered why the Messiah had not arrived in time to save them from The Holocaust. Then, according to Dr Fackenheim, they made a great leap of understanding, recognized that they had undergone the ultimate test and, not without anguish, accepted that it is precisely because it is now too late to expect the Messiah that they are commanded to hope.

The Covenant still survives. Every orthodox Jew one encounters after Auschwitz is the embodiment of hope breathtaking in its persistence.

It is not for the Christian who never experienced the terror and despair of Auschwitz to draw a conclusion different from that of his Jewish brethren. But he might, with the greatest diffidence and utmost humility, at least wonder whether the Messiah was not, in fact, present at Auschwitz, using the deportment of the Jews themselves in the years following The Holocaust to refute their own argument. Not only did most of them find the courage to live again but some went to great lengths to demonstrate that they had forgiven their enemies. It was the secular State of Israel and not religious Jewry which executed the grey-faced little clerk, Eichmann, who almost destroyed a whole Race merely by doing as he was told.

At a deeper level yet, universalist Jews and Christians are at one in acknowledging that God in Judgement is at odds with all peoples. Not even the enormity of the suffering of the Jews at Auschwitz can atone for the sinfulness they share with those who tormented them and with all mankind. I do not find such a rigorous doctrine palatable, yet it is some of the most profound Jewish thinkers who survived The Holocaust who claim Auschwitz as a supreme example of the solidarity of human guilt which renders void all distinctions between torturers and victims, guards and prisoners, executioners and executed. Hence, they declare, the only adequate Jewish response to The Holocaust is repentance; not vengeance nor self-pity – but repentance.

113

Here is surely a miracle of God's grace that those of us who never wore the Star of Judah on prison uniform can only salute in awed silence.

Auschwitz is often cited as the supreme monument to Man's bestiality towards his fellows. But something else was demonstrated there too – the truth that the commandment to hope gives a man the power to resist glaring evil, and imbues him with the strength to build a new humanity from the ruins of a broken body and a shattered family.

So when the Christian in Little Muddlecome-in-the-Mire thinks all is lost because the ecclesiastical scene looks so bleak, he needs an understanding Jewish friend to whisper in his ear, 'Don't you dare lose hope! God still reigns because *you* still believe!'

Perchance to Dream

Much attention is given by psychologists and their ilk to our night-dreams, but they show little interest in our day-dreaming. Indeed, day-dreaming is generally regarded as the disreputable preoccupation of born escapists seeking to evade the demands of stern reality. The very term conjures up a picture of some Dickensian clerk, perched on his high stool in a gloomy office, neglecting his work whilst he soars in imagination to an exotic foreign clime where dragons wait to be slain and lovely ladies are there for the wooing – until he is brought back to earth by a cuff about the ears from his boss. Dickens himself, like all successful fiction writers, could day-dream to his heart's content without condemnation because he made money out of the practice. Our society will always accord respect to whatever is economically profitable.

The Dickensian clerk is, of course, a victim of flagrant class discrimination. If he were an aircraft designer, poised over a drawing board, gazing blankly at the wall, oblivious of the racket going on around him, he would be hailed as a visionary rather than excoriated as a pathetic escapist. Yet both are engaged in a fundamental human activity – plotting alternative scenarios for the future. Such image-making is more than a pleasant diversion; it is the first stage in changing society. Reality has no fixed size. It is not nailed down, shut up, tied in a bundle. Only a fraction of the total human possibilities have been explored, and the first step in that operation is to give house-room in the mind to an image, become intoxicated by it and then put it to the test of practicability.

Historically, the great thinkers who have embodied their visions of the future in works of literature have invariably been Utopian in the sense that they have seen Man's tomorrows as an infinite improvement on his past – Plato, Thomas More, Francis Bacon, Campanella, Fourier and St Simon – all described worlds in which freedom and virtue were enthroned and evil banished. It is a symptom of the more sombre mood of our time that the two best known fictional representations of Mankind's future – Orwell's *1984* and Aldous Huxley's *Brave New World* predict the victory of totalitarianism and the de-humanizing of Man.

It is the writers of science fiction who now have a virtual monopoly in projections of the future of the human race. A few treat their trade with deadly seriousness; most indulge in fantasy magnified to cosmic proportions. Such work has entertainment value, but it is little help in planning a good future.

There is one question which must tantalize those who are prepared to accept some degree of personal responsibility for the shape of the future. Are the boundaries of the future limited by the range of the human imagination? Is anything possible that Man just couldn't imagine? Christianity is the short answer. Alone amongst world religions, it tells of events which no human brain could possibly predict as hap-

115

pening within history. Its key-concepts – Incarnation, Atonement, Resurrection and Consummation – are not historically imaginable. Certainly there are religions which describe virgin births and dying and rising Gods, but they make no claim that these imponderables are anything other than *myths*. Christianity, on the other hand, insists that just such events actually happened, are happening or are destined to happen within history – a mind-boggling contention if ever there was one. So Christian hope is without any limits the human imagination might place upon it.

But neither religion nor literature have the copyright on futurology any longer. The scientists have stepped in and are busy projecting present trends into the future and offering Mankind a selection of possible tomorrows. The archpriest of this cult is Herman Kahn who, together with Anthony Wiener, has written a book *The Year 2000* which tabulates dozens of possible human destinies. Man can choose his future from amongst a series of alternatives that are, in effect, visions fleshed out in scientific and political form. It is not an easy book to read; the jargon-quotient is formidable. But it is an important work if only because it calls the Church's bluff. We are playing precisely the same game. Are not many of our strategies of evangelism, our manpower policies and much of our theology based upon a systematic form of day-dreaming – imaginative projections of what the future of the Church is likely to be? The American theologian, Martin E. Marty, has sketched out a number of possible scenarios for the future of Christianity and shown how our ecclesiastical policies and personal faith are influenced by them.[19]

There is the *Triumph Game* which assumes the restoration of some form of the long-vanished Christendom when the Church wielded great secular power. Since God is sovereign, his Church must eventually *win*. Let the heathen mock and the atheist sneer, God will re-establish the

116

Church in its former glory. Statistics of declining church membership are brushed aside, all the evidences of defeat are illusory. The triumphalist believes it to be his vocation to go on going on, perpetuating the attitudes and policies of his fathers. He is an unapologetic advocate of the grand irrelevance of the Church. There is no reason why he should accommodate his theology, hymnody and preaching to the culture and mood of the day. If the masses find the Gospel unintelligible and church-going a waste of time, then so much the worse for them. The Church *must* win because it is of supernatural origin and so cannot be destroyed by any earthly power. That the New Testament talks much more of the humiliation and suffering of the Church than of its victory, the triumphalist ascribes to the cultural shock of the early Christians when the world failed to end on cue.

An alternative scenario is the *Defeat Game*, played by the Christian who shares many of the attitudes of the triumphalists but who, yoga-like, stands on his head in a corner and sees everything upside down. Every sign of the Church's decline is evidence of approaching victory. Losses in membership are not only to be expected but demonstrate that the Church is really doing its job. His favourite text is, 'Where two or three are gathered together in my name, I am there in the midst', and he can't get to that point quickly enough. He is a theological masochist whose desire to be humiliated is almost pathological. In extreme cases, the defeatist would welcome the complete disappearance of the Church as a social phenomenon, so that a fresh start could be made, not in some great cathedral but in the sitting room of his council house. The contention of some conservative theologians that the Church is prior to all else in Christianity; that the New Testament authors wrote not only to the Church but out of it, he brushes aside with contempt. He wants to scrape off the accumulated barnacles of two thousand years of Church history and get back to Jesus. That is

117

the ideal working unit for the salvation of the world – himself, a couple of friends, and Jesus.

The third scenario is *retrench*. Let Christians stand firm, keep cool and ride out the storm. By all means the Church should rid itself of whatever is obviously antiquated in its life and structures, but history is cyclic; what has been, will be again. The important thing is to guard jealously a deposit of Faith against radical theologians or godless critics. The datum line is some period in the Church's past when similarly unpropitious conditions prevailed. By all means bend a little to meet the mood of the times – a modicum of liturgical reform, a *soupçon* of trendy preaching, a touch of radicalism (the odd Christian Aid exhibition does no one any harm), a colloquial version of the Bible in public worship – all these are permissible, given congregational support. Church structures might, with advantage, be given a facelift, ignoring that dictum of the business world that the final act of a dying organization is to produce a revised and enlarged edition of the rule book. But the key theme is majestically simple and not too onerous – Hang On!

A fourth scenario is *Adapt* – get with it! The catchphrase is: 'Let the world write the Agenda.' The Church ought not to stand out from the terrain like a giraffe but merge into the landscape like a chameleon. Any doctrine likely to stick in the world's gizzard should be jettisoned; any symbolism not immediately intelligible to the man in the street is pointless and counter-productive. Two examples will serve to summarize this strategy, one concerning the Church's architecture, the other, the communication of the Gospel. The rationale behind the building of Methodist Central Halls at the turn of the century was the fact that people flocked to theatres and cinemas so it might pay to get rid of the churchy atmosphere of the place of worship, replace the pews with tip-up seats, the pulpit with a platform and possibly import an orchestra to take the place of
118

the organ. Then the man in the street might not find the transition from cinema to church too jarring. This is not to say that Methodist Central Halls did not and do not offer splendid service to their local communities, though it is interesting that most of those recently renovated have become much more ecclesiastical in style. The other example of the *Adaption* scenario concerns T.V. religion, where the programme 'Stars on Sunday' is based upon the assumption that viewers who watch 'Saturday Variety' will find a sacred version of the same format more palatable than hard-line Christianity.

Possibly the most positive scenario is that of *Reform*. Bring to bear the best scholarship upon Christian theology and the Bible, return to the Reformers or go even further back to the Early Fathers for the material of devotion and the style of apologetic. Listen with attentive ears to what the Spirit is saying to the Church from sources both sacred and secular, and obey it. Drastically reduce the Church's plant and structures so that they are manageable and do not absorb an inordinate amount of time and money that ought to be spent not upon domestic housekeeping but on the world for which the Church exists. It is the rediscovery of the Servant-Church, severely functional and testing the totality of its activities against the standard – do they do the job?

This is a realistic scenario because it recognizes the simple truth that the Church can only be reformed; it cannot be revolutionized. There is about any institution two thousand years old a massive degree of inertia – in the strictest sense of that word. The young bloods who dream of turning the Christian community into a radical pressure group are crying for the moon. The Church is, and always has been, a conservative body which has, from time to time, thrown up radical movements. The Reformers, Wesley, William Booth, may have struck off in new directions, but they were

119

the children of a conservative organization, which might be moved an inch or two to the Left but cannot be turned inside out and upside down.

The final scenario is that of *Risk*. The demand of those who follow through this script is that the Church should realize all her assets and give them to the poor; that she ought to stake everything upon denying herself any future and explode in a great burst of compassion for Mankind, leaving it to God to raise up witnesses should he desire them when the dust has settled. The theological model upon which the Risk-Taker bases his policy of utter abandon is the Death and Resurrection of Jesus. If the Church should die as a result of following the way of Jesus, she is assured of Resurrection, though in what form no man can say.

What cannot be denied is that there is an element of truth in each one of these scenarios, yet there seems no prospect of combining them to construct a strategy for the future. For at root, we are dealing with the conditioning of history and the limited malleability of human temperament. Any Church that can contain both Billy Graham and Reinhold Niebhur, Albert Schweitzer and Martin Luther King, William Temple and Dick Sheppard, Mother Teresa and Pope Paul IV is both a mystery and a mess – a great, sprawling, untidy organism whose centre is fixed but whose circumference is impossible to define. And that's as it should be. For in the last resort, only Christ knows his own.

My own preference for a scenario combines two elements within the Church presently at odds, dividing one Christian from his brother with a greater degree of bitterness than any Denominational barrier could generate. It is the *Traditional Radical* tension which has inflicted deep and lasting wounds upon the Church through sheer inability to recognize that, should either party win, the Church is doomed. If the traditionalist succeeds in driving out the radical then the Church's thinking will have become fossilised in the 4th century. On the other hand, should the radical prevail, the Church will be at the mercy of every passing whim and fancy of contemporary culture.

The only way forward for the Church is one that avoids the Either-Or of traditionalist or radical thinking and holds both together in a tension softened by mutual charity. The truth is that both traditionalist and radical need each other to prevent them from falling into monstrous error.

The radical needs the traditionalist because he operates on that dangerous boundary between Faith and Unfaith and it is inevitable that he will occasionally get hopelessly lost. Hence, he needs to be able to return to a core of traditional Christianity from which he can set out again to take his stand alongside the anonymous Christ who is at work in the secular world. The radical also needs roots, though he may not appreciate the fact. It is an illusion that one can wipe out one's past and begin again from scratch, short-circuiting two thousand years of Christian history in order to project oneself backwards to a time and place where Christ lived and taught, suffered and died, rose and ascended. The radical can locate his roots in Marxism or Humanism or in any other ideology, but only at the price of ceasing to be a *Christian* radical. He can mediate goodness, compassion humanity, but he cannot mediate Christ from any other source than the gnarled and tangled roots of the historical Christian community. And the radical needs too the support of the traditional Christian's office of Intercession. It is the fact that the world is being prayed for, offered up to God constantly, which enables the radical to change it.

By the same token, the traditionalist needs the radical. For it is only through the dangerous explorations of the radical that the traditionalist has any way forward into the future. Otherwise he is imprisoned in the past like a man whose feet are stuck in concrete. And without the radical's

121

insistence upon taking the world with the utmost seriousness, the traditionalist becomes obscurantist, performing rituals that have long since lost any meaning. He can offer only other men's prayers in language which cuts him off from engagement with the contemporary world. Most serious of all, without the witness of the radical, the traditionalist abandons self-questioning and mouths dogmas which are the mouldering corpse of dead prophecy. He may have a sure grasp of what Jesus has done, but he has no knowledge of that new thing which Jesus is doing in the life of this time.

Is there anything more than mutual tolerance that can hold traditionalist and radical together? The answer is that both are committed to the search for a new society. No traditionalist who *listens* to the words which pour out of his mouth every time he utters the Lord's Prayer or says the Daily Office can evade the sharp challenge expressed in the comforting language of the past. He *must* see that whilst it may be necessary to sacrifice the present for the future, Biblical religion will not allow him to sacrifice the present to the past. God is not content with our present society – that is the message which comes across loud and clear in the most traditional liturgy. That is not to say that God will be more content with any society which replaces the present one. Traditional Christianity baptizes no doctrine of secular progress. The Kingdom of God is not the final move in some endless chess game. It comes from beyond history, cleaving it in two and commanding the Christian, whatever his theological position, to stand by and for it. So the traditionalist and the radical are committed to the same task, though they may take it up at different points.

Possibly what I am describing is the apparently contradictory role of every Christian as both prophet and priest. Not the tension between the prophets and priests in the Church – that is a squabble with an honourable ancestry stretching back to Moses and Aaron – but the tension between the prophet and priest in each Christian. Every Christian is the servant of an historical Word in the sense that it refers to unrepeatable events concerned with a Life and Work which is complete and sealed for ever, and it is the priestly role to preserve the record of those events and rehearse them within the Church. But this Word is also an Apostolic Word which needs new voices and accents to tell it forth in every time as God's response to the questions any Age formulates – and this is a prophetic function.

In Old Testament times, the currents of thought generated by prophet and priest sometimes converged, diverged, ran parallel or more often collided.[20] Prophetic obedience is to a vision. He has a clear duty to urge the people forward into the unknown. The priest has an equally plain duty to preserve the people from taking an irretrievable step that will lead them to disaster. The priest names the name of Jesus who is for ever the Christ, Lord and Saviour. The prophet takes his stand by the Jesus who is known within history by many names or none.

If the tension between priest and prophet was acute in Biblical times, how much more crucial does it become in the modern Church where the Christian must discharge both priestly and prophetic functions alike, whether he is ordained or lay? It is this tension, not of our making but characteristic of Biblical religion, which is the real cause of the traditional/radical division. It is pointless either pretending that no tension exists or that we can adopt a truly Biblical stance by standing for one and opposing the other. There is in every Christian's faith, prophetic and priestly elements, in varying proportions. And the reality of things is expressed in that tension which threatens to tear each of us apart, let alone divide us from our fellow-Christian who through temperament and experience, puts greater weight upon a different aspect of the same many-faceted truth.

The only way of avoiding a rising tide of bitterness which must negate the very Gospel itself can only be by the exercise of charity – the willingness to bless ministries which we cannot temperamentally endorse but which have been manifestly blessed by God. To take a specific example, my own theology is light-years removed from that of Dr Billy Graham, but it is my Christian duty to do everything possible to strengthen his witness and avoid undermining his work by destructive criticism. By the same token, I have no right to expect Dr Graham to endorse my theology, but I would hope to receive his charitable understanding when I try to do God's will according to my sincere apprehension of it. Let the theological debate rage as it has done from the dawn of the Christian Era, but within a framework of mutual tolerance and charity. It is only in this spirit that God's work is going to get done.

Let etymology have the last word. The radical believes his orientation is towards the future, yet the term *radical* has a backward reference to the search for roots. The conservative believes he is the guardian of all that is of value in the Church's past, but the term *conservative* means preserving whatever is essential for a good future.

Where, then, does hope lie in this wounding conflict which has led to so much blood-letting in the Church? Surely in the obvious fact that neither radical nor conservative is likely to convert the other to his own position. Instead, he must recognize that the bias of a fellow-Christian's theology is not half so important as the use to which he puts the theology he holds. No Christian, no theological school, no branch of the Church can contain and express the plenitude of Christian hope. Yet each Christian must add his own bit to the rest. To withhold it is a mortal sin.

What effect the radical/conservative theological tension expressed in Christian charity might have upon the future of the Church, it is impossible to predict. But if the New Testament is taken seriously, then Christian Mission will be seen as an act of Grace rather than an investment. And it is the nature of God's Grace that it is poured out regardless of the return it receives. Whether that truth spells hope or doom for the Church only God knows, and he has a habit of keeping to himself many things we would dearly love to be certain of. For should all God's truth be revealed within history, what is the point of faith at all?

Dare We Hope for Miracles?

In describing the Clown as a symbol of hope, I ranged my-self firmly on the side of those who believe in Gospel mira-cles. I didn't develop the subject; my comments were a mere aside. But I can't leave matters there. For some would say that hope is pointless unless we are permitted to pray for things which would normally be regarded as impossible. Who needs to be told that this whole area of Christian be-lief bristles with more difficulties than a porcupine has quills? There are some great themes about which the Church has maintained a magnificent consistency through-out the Ages, never wavering about a core of reality that might need putting in different words as fashions in culture and language change. But such accommodations hadn't the motive of making that reality believable, they sought only to render it intelligible. Christian thinking about miracles has, however, been decidedly fuddled.

There are those who accept without question that miracles took place two thousand years ago in the Middle East but will snort with derision at the possibility that one occurred in the next street last week. There are Protestants who view with dark suspicion claims by the Roman Catholic Church that miracles have been performed by her saints throughout Christian history. Granted, some of these events called mir-acles seem such crude and arbitrary breaches of the laws of

125

Nature that to take them seriously is to project oneself backwards into the world of witches, spells and exorcism. Catholics, on the other hand, find the determination of some Protestants to accept Scriptural miracles and no others, as fundamentalism of the worst sort and, what is more serious, to imply belief in a God who shut up shop when the final full-stop was put to the last book of the Bible.

The whole issue is bedevilled by problems of definition. One man's miracle is another man's scientific fact. I have heard a devout naval Captain argue that the sudden abatement of the seas during the evacuation of the British Army from the Dunkirk beaches in 1940 was an answer to prayer, and grow puce with rage when an agnostic meterologist countered with an explanation of what to him was a perfectly normal phenomenon, with diagrams to prove his point. The easy way out is to rule that both were right – God operated through a natural process to answer prayer. One might with greater difficulty use the same trick to explain an older and odder event. According to the Second Book of Kings, an invasion by Senacherib was halted by angels. The Greek historian, Herodotus, telling the same story, ascribes the frustration of Senacherib's intentions to an incursion of mice who ate up the bow-strings of his archers. Now if you are prepared to widen your definition of angels as 'non-human agents of God' to include mice, then it is possible to harmonize the two accounts of the same event. But such mental acrobatics duck the real issue, which is wrapped up in the question: does God actively intervene in history and if necessary suspend his own laws in response to the prayers of the believer?

My own generation's thinking on the subject of miracles was conditioned by the massive intellect of C. S. Lewis, who never baulked at tackling a difficult subject and whose mastery of language made his explanations seem deceptively simple. His impatience with Biblical scholars such as

Rudolf Bultmann laid him open to the charge that he was highly selective in his use of the New Testament in order to make the Christian Faith more acceptable to the man in the street. But since I wish to make only one point about miracles and therefore intend to take the lazy man's way out and avoid analysing each of the Gospel miracles, I find Lewis' treatment of the subject both ingenious and helpful.[21]

Two conditions are necessary to make sense of miracles, Scriptural or otherwise, a recognition of the stability of the Natural and a belief in the Supernatural. It is nonsense, for instance, to claim that our ancestors believed in miracles because they were ignorant of the laws of Nature. For unless you have some idea of what is normal, how can you describe anything as abnormal? If this distinction is beyond you, then you are, to put it mildly, in a mess. Either you will regard *anything* as normal, from crops growing to trees walking, or else you will blithely accept that everything is abnormal in the sense that it is an event attributable to the direct action of whatever gods you happen to believe in. Lewis makes this point by giving two examples from the Gospels. Then Joseph found out that Mary was pregnant, he was 'minded to put her away'. Obviously he knew enough biology to attribute pregnancy to intercourse with some man. And when he accepted the classical Christian explanation of Mary's condition, he assumed a miracle because he knew enough about the laws of Nature to see that this event was a suspension of them. In the same way, the disciples were frightened when they saw Jesus walking on the water towards them because they were aware that it wasn't a normal thing for someone to do. And if fishermen didn't know that it wasn't possible to walk on water, who would?

Miracles are a way of telling men something about the relationship between God and his world. And as such, they fall into two broad categories, though there is the odd miracle which refuses to be neatly pigeon-holed. There are miracles of the Old Order, which by the method of speeding up the camera, as it were, dramatize things that God is doing all the time but which men foolishly take for granted. The turning of water into wine at Cana of Galilee is an obvious example. God is always turning water into wine. The vine draws up water from its roots, and with the aid of the sun, ferments that juice into an essence we call wine. Since time immemorial this natural process has gone on at a pace governed by the cycle of the seasons. But when Jesus does the same thing in a moment of time, men are shocked into an awareness of God's creative providence that they are otherwise prone to take for granted. Another classical case is the feeding of the Five Thousand. All the wheat which is reaped in thousands of tons throughout the American heartlands originated in a handful of seeds, barely sufficient to fill an envelope. A little produces a lot, and goes on reproducing still more. This is a fact of Nature which only impinges upon Man's consciousness because Jesus altered the time-scale of the process. As with the bread, so also the fish. A jar-full of tiny creatures sparks off an explosion of fecundity in seas and rivers.

It is important to note that Jesus did not create the bread and fishes which satisfied the crowd's hunger either from nothing or from some alien matter such as the stone which the Devil offered him at the Temptation. The five loaves and two small fishes were not theatrical props. They were the essential preconditions of the miracle. Only God can create something out of nothing, as he did at the Creation. Jesus needed a basic working material of the same order as that which was the essence of the miracle. The Son cannot do everything the Father has done, otherwise he would be a manifestation of an independent Divinity, and the whole Christian doctrine of God would degenerate into some form of polytheism.

Most of the Healing miracles demonstrate the same point.

The wise physician who declared of a patient, 'God healed him; I merely dressed his wounds' showed a scientific humility which contrasts with the almost superstitious credulity the general public displays towards the medical profession. God made men whole in a good Creation. And more often than not, what we call medicine either stimulates the processes of natural healing or combats the forces which seek to hinder those processes. Hence, all men are cured by the Healer within. But a re-creative process that is constantly taking place was laid bare to human sight by Jesus when he healed the sick.

Such miracles are fundamental parables of Creation. They spell out and underline truths which Man is disposed to take for granted until he is brought up short against them in an act dramatic enough to engage his attention. These miracles are quite different from the extraordinary happenings of which we might read in Ovid's *Metamorphoses* or Grimm's *Fairy Tales*, where purely random impossibilities occur such as trees talking, men changing into snakes or bears; where stones in fact can become bread at the whim of some rogue God, who because he is not bound by the laws he himself has made, can do anything, however intrinsically absurd. In a world ruled by such a supernatural despot, men would be at the mercy of pure arbitrariness. God would be like the irrational school-master who doles out favours or awards punishments on grounds so trivial as the fact that he woke up one morning with a headache and the next with a song in his heart.

The Gospels, however, record a second class of miracles which foretell what God has not yet done but will do universally some day. Such miracles are parables of the New Creation. God raised Jesus from the dead as a promise, or a warning, depending upon your viewpoint, of a time when he will raise all men from the dead. The Transfiguration of Jesus on the Mount of Olives is a pre-view of what the New

Humanity will look like. Jesus walking upon water is symbolic of an era when all men who walk with God will have effortless power over matter, sustained by a new force driving through and beyond the realm of the natural. And the man born blind has his eye-sight restored to demonstrate that some day all men will see the world in its pristine glory, restored to what it was before evil marred and scarred it.

But as the New Testament Epistles are at pains to point out, we live between the Times, and so there are miracles which span the gap between the Old and New Creations. They cannot be fitted neatly into either category. The raising of Lazarus or Jairus' daughter from the dead are not miracles of the same order as the Resurrection of Jesus because both are restored to their former state. Mortality is still woven into their nature and an irreversible natural death lies ahead of them. These miracles are strictly inexplicable except as evidences that the power of irresistible love can breakout of the sphere of the New Creation and upset the patterns and laws of the Old Creation. They are practical proof of the truth that the Natural and Supernatural are not carefully separated orders of being. The Supernatural penetrates the Natural at so many points that the odd mortal may find himself at the juxtaposition of the two, like the man who is sheltering under the one tree in a whole forest which lightning strikes.

Glory insists on breaking in upon the Natural Order, and for an instant, men to their bewilderment, do not know who or what they really are. Lazarus or Jairus' daughter, when the Glory has departed, resume their natural state in the Old Order, because, historically, the New Order cannot come into being until Jesus is raised from the dead. But their restoration to the world of people who live and love and die is not without its symbolic significance. They are like lone birds winging across the grey skies of the Arctic winter – heralding the approach of Summer.

130

I take the Gospel miracles seriously, and the possibility of contemporary miracles equally seriously because it seems to me that in a world where the Supernatural inter-penetrates the Natural, *anything* which is not intrinsically absurd, anything that is in accord with the will of a loving Father, is possible.

There is no defence in the Natural world against miracles. Since Nature is only a tiny part of reality, she cannot erect barriers against invasion by powers greater than herself. If the sheer momentum of Divine love bursts into the world of human affairs, seeking out and enfolding whatever and whoever is starved of love, it is equally pointless to look for a natural explanation as to assume that the laws of Nature have been finally transcended. This world is no clock-work orange, which has the precision of some great, unbreakable machine and where cause and effect are precisely related. It is a wild thing of beauty and terror, horror and pity, poetry and fire, and so does not operate according to the laws of exact moral transactions, where good is rewarded by happiness and evil by misery. There is a rogue element in life. You may call it the Supernatural, the non-rational or the not-as-yet explained, according to your taste. But it is this strictly unpredictable dimension which makes tragedy inevitable but also miracles possible.

So whether miracles are an insult to human intelligence or overwhelming demonstrations of its limitations depends upon the view you take of a reality much further back – the ultimate intention of the Creator. If I were a novelist telling the story of a butcher's family in Barnsley and got the plot into such a mess that I was forced to turn the villain into a toad in order to write a final chapter that made any sense, then I would have broken the rules of good art, introducing an arbitrary wonder to bridge the gap created by my lack of artistic imagination. The same is true of miracles. Not even God can perform them in order to get his plot back

131

on track should his grand design prove to be based upon an absurdity. The analogy is useful. It is perfectly proper to introduce a ghost into a ghost story, but not into a Western; I can invent a planet unknown to astronomers if I am writing science-fiction but I cannot land an aeroplane on Deal Beach if I am a historical novelist telling how the Romans first landed in Britain near Dover around 55 BC.

If the Christian story were like one of those awful adventure serials of my childhood, where one chapter ended with the hero chained to the wall of a dungeon slowly being flooded by the sea, and the next chapter began . . . 'With one bound, our hero freed himself and caught a cab back to his Baker Street flat . . .', then I would not believe in miracles if all the Fathers of the Early Church swore affidavits testifying to their truth. But the Christian story is predicated upon one Grand Miracle – the Incarnation, and has another as its lynch-pin – the Resurrection. If I can swallow that lot, and I do, then I would expect lesser miracles to occur from time to time because they are entirely in keeping with the Author's intention. They are straws in the wind, pointers to the general drift of the plot.

Therefore, when someone enquires whether it is permissible to hope for a miracle, the short answer must be that it doesn't make sense to hope for anything else. For if something can be reasonably predicted; if a desirable future happening is grounded in a rational probability, then we have ceased to talk about hope. We are in the realm of sanctified common-sense, which is a perfectly respectable Christian virtue, but has as little to do with hope as a tipster betting on a race that has already been run, or more correctly, has still to be run but has only one horse in it, plus a donkey with a wooden leg.

You would expect some qualification, and here it is. It is not permissible to hope for a miracle of the kind which would turn a sow's ear into a silk purse. To request God to give you the looks of Elizabeth Taylor or the football skill of George Best does not fall within the rules governing miracles. In each case one is asking, not for the impossible but for the trivial – a purely arbitrary interference with Nature in order to get selfish advantage or private gratification. The miracles for which one can legitimately hope are those which bring your request into line with God's ultimate intention. Anything less would reduce God to the status of the African chief who for the space of one day in the year grants the petitions of tribesman, whatever they may be, who have performed some feat of great difficulty or danger.

But the Christian need not be intimidated by the stern moralist who scoffs that he has little respect for a God who over-rules his own laws in response to a human plea. He should ponder this simple truth. The laws of Nature have never yet produced a single event, miraculous or otherwise. They describe the pattern to which any event must conform, but they have no power to get that event to happen in the first place. I can, by the rules of arithmetic, work out to the nearest penny what income tax I shall have to pay on my salary, but the Inland Revenue will not accept my calculations in lieu of the actual money owed them. The Law of Gravity can describe what will happen to me if I jump from the top of Blackpool Tower; it can even calculate the speed at which I will hit the ground. But that Law cannot cause me to jump in the first place. Hence, when the Christian talks of hope he is not making predictions on the basis of any Natural Laws. He is doing something much more fundamental. He is putting his trust in the Source of those events, which *once they occur* will, in general, conform to a pattern we call the Natural Order. But at root, Christian hope has to do with the mystery of a Mighty Will at work in, through and occasionally in spite of the Laws of Nature.

Need one add that though it is permissible to hope for a miracle, it is both foolhardy and sub-Christian to build a philosophy of life upon the assumption that God will bend the Laws of Nature in our favour whenever the going gets tough. For this would destroy our human dignity and reduce us to puppets on a string. And puppets don't need to hope. They can only respond to the next jerk. In fact, they are moral and spiritual non-beings not only because they do not need to hope, but because they have nothing to hope for.

Not Only – But Also

I had better rid myself of an uneasy feeling in my bones that some reader is going to pole-axe me with the obvious and justifiable criticism that I have rambled on and on about hope as though it were a quality existing in splendid isolation, a single virtue powerful enough to fuel the engine of a dynamic Christian life. Let me quickly pass the buck and protest that I, like many other run of the mill parsons, have been seduced by those wicked theologians who keep the religious presses solvent and the theological faculties humming with their industry and mental fecundity. The trouble is that as their thoughts get more profound so the books which contain them get costlier. In the 1950s, five bobs' worth of John Robinson's *Honest to God* held pride of place on my shelves only to be dispossessed in the 1960s by Harvey Cox's *Secular City* at a quid a time. Now in the 1970s, I have been forced to choose between four tins of pipe tobacco and Johannes Moltmann's *Theology of Hope*. I made the great sacrifice only to find that whenever I try to read more than two paragraphs of Germanic density, my eye-lids slowly fold in sleep. This, I hasten to add, is no reflection on either Dr Moltmann or his book. I'm just so tired dashing around all day being hopeful that I haven't any stamina left to read about the subject.

It was, I suppose, inevitable that theologies of hope should proliferate in a Church whose nerve is cracking and
134

whose membership is declining at an alarming rate. Nor is it entirely coincidental that the Marxists should be hailing thinkers like Ernst Bloch as prophets of secular hope. The Communist Party in Britain is doing little better at the polls than we do at Parish communion. The more cynical observers of the current Marxist-Christian dialogue claim to detect about it the funereal air of two dying men making arrangements to occupy one grave. Even our most sympathetic onlookers might be forgiven for likening Marxist-Christian conversations about hope to the bankrupt Irishman's proposal that it would be a good idea for him to add his debts to those of his mate so that they would both be twice as rich.

Too intensive a concentration upon hope tends to encourage mellontolatry, which, to save you looking it up in the dictionary, means the worship of the future – a philosophy which tempts us to self-congratulation by enthroning the tautology that runs: we have almost reached our destination, and then defines our destination as the place we have almost reached. The New Testament offers a number of defences against mellontolatry, the most effective of which is to avoid isolating hope from its invariable companions – faith and love. These are not random virtues practised by the Christian. They are the essential, inter-locking dimensions of the Christian life, which is defective if it neglects any of the three. *Hope* is possible because the one who follows the way of Christ has *faith* that there is no situation which is impervious to *love*. Here are the three pillars upon which the Kingdom of God is raised – faith venturing beyond the unprovable, love forgiving the unpardonable, and hope remaining expectant against all odds. Chop away any one of those three supports and the Kingdom crashes in ruins.

Each of these three dimensions of the Christian life is not only dependent upon the other two, but is also specific ra-

135

ther than general, precise rather than vague, anchored in a particular historical moment rather than mingling in some time-less wisdom. The human component in faith is obedience; in hope, utter availability; in love, 'letting be' – all in, through and because of Jesus. And each of these three march together, marking out the tracks of the Kingdom. A Church without hope is as inconceivable as a Church without faith and as powerless as a Church without love. Whatever its shortcomings and failures, the Church is the one place where on earth these three abiding realities are made visible to the eyes of men.

When Paul assures us that 'Now abide faith, hope, love . . .', he is describing both a sequence of events and an order of priorities. *Love* is God's love coming to us in Christ; *faith* is our surrender to that love; and *hope* is the expectation that the God who has given us so much, will in the end give us all things, or at least, all the things we need to fulfil our humanity. Love and faith have greater importance than hope. God's love is given to us in Christ – that is a dead certainty; faith as our recognition and acceptance of this love is obviously next in order of importance; and hope is still essential but cannot have the same degree of certainty as the other two, otherwise the word would have lost all meaning. We *hope* for heaven – for the life of the world to come. If hope has the same status as faith and love, then it would render both of them unnecessary. Love would become simply Divine power because it could not be resisted, and this in turn would mean the annulment of Man's freedom to say 'No' to God to the end. Faith would harden into a certainty which rendered unbelief impossible or insane. For who in his right mind need have faith in what has been proved beyond a shadow of a doubt? Hence, though hope is lowest in the hierarchy of theological virtues, it adds tang to the rest, making the Christian life an adventure rather than an existence of mechanical certitude.

136

Just as hope must not be separated from its companion-virtues in the life of the Christian, so, too, its significance must not be confined to the dimension of the future. It has present relevance when it both points back to the past and forward to the future. One of the striking things about history is that the Christians who have done most for this earth are those whose eyes have been firmly fixed on Heaven – and by Heaven I am ignoring the mythological elements that make it seem an improbable as well as unattractive place, and use the term to mean the joy of the ultimate fulfilment of our humanity through union with God. By that reckoning, it has been Heaven-orientated Christians who have made a massive contribution to the betterment of the earth.

The Apostles set in motion the conversion of the Roman Empire – a saga of struggle, suffering and martyrdom. But to read their writings you would get the impression they were so preoccupied with the next world that they could not have been less interested in this one. Those Medieval monks, locked away in their great fortress-monasteries, had their time so taken up with prayer and meditation and other-worldly pursuits as to be totally cut off from the work-a-day life. Yet they laid the foundations of modern knowledge and were amongst the great architects of our civilization. And it was 18th-century Evangelicals who seemed so pious and ethereal that they might vapourize at any moment who were instrumental in abolishing slavery and child labour. Arguably the most powerful missionary force in Africa are the White Fathers who in the course of winning converts to the Christian Faith performed great feats of exploration, transformed the cultural life of the peoples amongst whom they worked and were implacable enemies of the Arab slavers. The examples are endless. At the turn of this century, there was barely a stinking stew of a city slum without an Anglo-Catholic priest whose churchmanship was so high it made the Nonconformists dizzy and yet he was a leader in social reform, thundering denunciation from his pulpit upon inhuman employers and vicious landlords.

It was, I think, C. S. Lewis, who charged that only since Christians have largely ceased to think of the other world have they become so ineffective in this. The rule seems to be that if you aim at Heaven, you will get earth 'thrown in'. Aim at earth and you will get neither. It is a strange rule, but can be demonstrated in many fields of life. Health is a great blessing, but let it become an obsession and you end up a crank and a hypochondriac. You only get health provided you want other things more – fun, food, games, work and open air.

The balancing truth about hope is that its future reference frees men from worldly despair when everything seems likely to crash about their ears. Fifteen hundred years ago, in the fifth century of our era, there lived and worked in the North African town of Hippo, a bishop who decisively moulded the thought of Western Christendom, so that the very core of our civilization bears the imprint of his genius. St Augustine lived in times of upheaval and ruin. Rome had just fallen to the Barbarians; and to Pagan and Christian alike, it seemed the end of all things. In the words of St Jerome, 'The light of the world had been put out'. To the materialist or the pleasure-seeker, nothing could be more futile than the spectacle of St Augustine busying himself with the reunion of the African Church and the refutation of the Pelagians, whilst civilization was falling to pieces about him. It seemed like the activity of an ant which works on whilst its nest is destroyed. But Augustine saw things otherwise. He looked beyond the aimless and bloody chaos of history to the world of eternal realities from which the world of sense derives all the significance it possesses.

Augustine went about his daily task as a bishop, trying in the face of the sternest adversity to cope with the predicaments of his time in the light of eternal principles. He went on thinking, writing and clarifying the principles and ideals which should guide individual and political life. The Church in Africa, to whose service he gave the later part of his life, was to be blotted out so completely as though it had never existed. St Augustine's age marked, in the words of Christopher Dawson, 'the failure of the greatest experiment in secular civilization the world has ever seen'.[22] Yet Augustine's faith was justified and his writings were to influence not only the Middle Ages but also the Reformers who appealed to his teaching against the Schoolmen. Indeed, without his massive intellect and spiritual perception Western theology would have been broken-backed. Yet from the viewpoint of 5th-century Hippo, he was the supreme unrealist, who would have been better occupied in fleeing from the wrath to come than in building what seemed to be a castle of cards in the teeth of a gale.

How desperate is the modern Church's need for a visionary who had Augustine's grasp of the sweep of history! His great prose epic, *The City of God*, begins with the fall of the rebellious angels and ends where men are glorified in the Beatific Vision of God. Here was a man who saw *beyond* the relentless persecution of the Church and indeed saw *in* the persecution of that Church not God's fortress going up in flames but as he put it in a famous sermon 'the brands scattering and the world being set on fire'.

This is the true nature of hope; that it gathers up past, present and future in one majestic vision, refusing to be imprisoned in one time or to take its datum point from any secular event, however terrifying or hopeful. It draws from past and present to feed the future. It projects back from the future a perspective that puts what has been and what is

139

firmly in their place as mere foot-notes to an epic that is beyond the imagination of Man to encompass. Certainly, Christian hope has its datum points in the past – Exodus and Easter, each of which describes an impossible possibility.

Exodus describes the free choice of a squad of Semitic slaves to opt for the desert, freedom and possibly death, rather than the servitude and security of Egypt. They start off bravely but soon reach a dead end, or to be more precise, an unbridgeable gulf – the Red Sea. I'm not prepared to get tangled up in arguments as to whether the parting of the Red Sea was a miraculous event or a natural phenomenon. It makes little difference. The important thing is that when those runaway slaves reached the end of their tether they discovered a totally unexpected saving possibility in an apparently hopeless situation. And they ascribed the miracle of their deliverance to their trust in a God whose nature is to transcend dead-ends. Has anyone a better explanation?

The other great datum point in the story of God's people is Easter where the hopes of a band of men who had caught a tantalizing glimpse of a new world were buried in a tomb with their leader. Yet again, at the end of their tether, they were presented with a totally unexpected saving possibility which unleashed new power and life into history.

So we cannot locate hope in one dimension or think of it as an isolated virtue. It is to be pictured more like a whirlwind that drives in all directions but ever upwards, rather than as a steady following breeze that blows the ship of faith always forward. In Dante's *Divine Comedy*, the poet sees hell, purgatory and paradise in one vision. So must the Christian, refusing to believe or to act as though the flux of events has finally deposited him once and for all in any one of the three. Within history, all three exist together. And it's a man of rare balance who can keep a cool head and a steady gait in such a whirling, dizzying time. But one thing is sure. The People of Exodus and Easter have no excuse for throwing in the towel and abandoning themselves to despair. It is both foolish and faithless to set limits on what the grace of God can accomplish.

Penultimate Ponderings

You have probably never heard of radio station KRML which serves the coastal resort of Carmel-by-the-Sea in California. I am told this little town is as near to the Garden of Eden as one is likely to get on earth. What makes Station KRML interesting is that until recently, and right up to the present day for all I know, its declared policy was to broadcast only what it termed 'Sunshine News'. Every morning, an announcer with a Happy-Happy voice would open the transmission with the words, 'Here is the good news of the world ...' and proceed to read a bulletin from which all mention of wars, tragedies and disasters were rigorously excluded. And in particular, Death was *Out*! Except for regrettable accidents, no one ever died in Carmel. Should a citizen contract a horrid disease, he made it a matter of honour to take himself off to some Los Angeles hospital or nursing home in which to expire. Civic pride indeed! though one might have reservations about the right of the citizens of Carmel to sweep the nasty bits of life under their expensive Persian carpets. They might retort that if they can afford the privilege of contracting out of the seamy side of existence, why shouldn't they? I could think of at least half a dozen answers to that one, but to spell them out would distract me from my main point which is that anyone who writes about hope is bound to find himself sooner or later on collision-course with the Grim Reaper. Then he wishes he'd never started the wretched book!

The academic theologian deals with Death as one ele-

141

ment in Eschatology – the study of the Last Things. For the working parson, it is an obscene reality with which he is required from time to time to wrestle not for the purposes of a Ph.D. thesis but in the antiseptic atmosphere of a hospital ward, by the bedside of a dying child. I have no desire to sound either condescending or scornful of academic theologians, most of whom have done pastoral duty at some stage in their careers. But they would be the first to admit, I suspect, that it is easier to speak of hope with a confident ring in the voice in the lecture room than at the grave-side. Even the physician who, God knows, sees more than his share of death, will often concede that the job of staving it off as long as possible and then certifying its cause, is less formidable than the parson's task of trying to explain to distracted relatives *why* it has happened.

Should the foregoing be taken as a 'plug' for the run-of-the-mill parson, so be it. He deserves one. His sense of humour can wear thin when he is constantly being thumped on the back by hearty hedonists who chuckle, 'You've got the best job of the lot, Vicar – one hour a week!' That hour doesn't take account of the times he has to drag himself out at night and dash down the corridors of the local hospital in time to hear the last words, or more terrifying, try to answer the anguished final question of the waxen-faced figure in the bed who heaves and sighs, and is no more.

The parson cannot avoid treating death with the utmost seriousness. No Christian, for example, can accept the Stoics' view that death is a matter of indifference – that someone who wasn't, *was* for a brief instant, and then wasn't any more. Equally, he rejects the contemporary secular-liberal view that death doesn't happen. Well, it happens all right, but always to someone else; that the dying patient must be constantly assured that he is getting better – the collective conspiracy of the nurses' cheery chat, the relatives' indefatigable determination to plan next year's
142

holiday for him, the doctor's deft evasion of the patient's pointedly hopeful questions about his condition.

Death's challenge to hope has to be assessed at a whole series of levels. At its lowest, death puts a person's life into a perspective free from illusion or false values. Take a practical instance from my own pastoral experience. Let's call him Fred, who, as the publisher's blurb almost says, bears every resemblance to most people, living and dead.

Fred's character was as drab as his life. He worked for the local council and rented a couple of rooms in one of London's dreariest streets. He lived alone but showed symptoms of neither loneliness nor self-sufficiency. He was not a proliterian roisterer nor a humble man of shining goodness, and suffered none of that dramatic poverty which would have had Shelter howling on his behalf for retribution to the God of Social Justice. If anyone loved him, they did not declare themselves at the funeral. He adored no scraggy mongrel or sleek cat; not even a pet canary to whom he could whisper secrets in the silence of the night.

In sum, Fred was prosaically rather than mysteriously anonymous. After his death, they did not find twenty thousand quid in old fivers under a pile of newspapers, nor even a bundle of faded letters, tear-stained and much-thumbed. Fred's position in the silent majority was dead-centre in the back row, biting his finger-nails. He did the Pools and had chance smiled on him, he would, no doubt, have ended his days in a dismal boarding house at a run-down seaside town, with distant relatives making anxious pilgrimage to see how his health fared.

He died of an indeterminate disease and did not suffer with any marked heroism.

The Russian philosopher Berdyaev wrote that every human soul has more meaning and value than the whole of history with its empires, wars and revolutions. I wonder what Berdyaev would have made of Fred? What secular philosopher could describe a cosmic system in which Fred had more than marginal significance? He breathed, occupied space, was there, and then was there no more. The flowers have withered on his grave and it is doubtful that the insurance money will both cover his funeral expenses and run to a tomb-stone.

Leaving aside for the moment the Christian revelation, society is divided between those who believe that death is the end and those who hope it isn't. I suppose the more sentimental humanist, surveying the awful aridity of Fred's life, might cast a tentative vote in favour of some world or dimension of existence in which Fred becomes *somebody* and does *something* which justifies the millions of years of evolutionary pain that went into his making.

The Christian affirmation of death takes up these bleak insights about Fred without attempting to romanticize them by replacing the withered flowers on his grave with those ghastly artificial wreaths under glass, waxen and curling at the edges, beloved of relatives who wish to save themselves the trouble of regular visits to the cemetery.

Fred, though he couldn't spell the word, let alone make a stab at guessing its meaning, was an ecological problem like the rest of us. We have to die to make room for generations still unborn who are entitled to their share of the finite resources of a planet slowly wasting away. That is, of course, a scientific rather than Christian insight, but none the less true for that. The right of my grand-children to have air to breathe, water to consume and space in which to live out their allotted span depends upon my death and that of my generation. That is what death is about at the most mundane level – human survival. Fred had to die in order that other Freds could be born, be they street sweepers or brain surgeons, Western play-boys or Indian peasants.

But that is not the whole story by any means. The tragedy

of Fred and millions like him, is not that he died, but that he barely lived. His death merely put terminus to his unlived life – moments empty of meaning, days dragged out by sheer monotony, weeks measured only by the handing-over of a pay packet or the dropping of a football pool coupon through the letter-box every Thursday, months marked out by changes in temperature, indicated by the frequency with which shillings had to be dropped in the gas meter, years that the locusts ate – the waning of natural appetites, the slowing of mental processes, the extra effort required to climb those dingy stairs.

Death is not only the revelation of unlived life, it is also a process well-described by A. N. Whitehead as 'perpetual perishing'. I know an Indian tailor in Zambia who has a clever party trick. He takes a bowl of water and sprinkles coloured dust on its placid surface, creating not only landscapes but also crude portraits of someone present. Then he blows on the water and the pattern dissolves in a multicoloured swirl. What is interesting about his performance is that he will never repeat it exactly. All the gold in Fort Knox won't entice him to sketch the same face twice. 'He's gone!' he mutters morbidly, and passes on to the next subject. His artistry is somewhat crude but his theology is sound. Death is not a future event but a present reality. Not only is it true that from the moment of our birth we are dying cell by cell but there is an inexorable movement of all our experiences, feelings and thoughts into some void, for ever beyond our reach in a past becoming increasingly remote. This truth puts into gloomy perspective all theories of perpetual suvival, whether of some spark that remains unextinguished by the exhaustion of our natural life-fuel or of a soul that leaves a worn-out organism to take up residence in another. What is the point of endless life if its net result is nothing?

Both Jewish and Greek thought reflect the fear of joyless

145

existence beyond death. Sheol or Hades are places of exile, where bloodless wraiths are cut off not only from humanity but also from the fullness of life emanating from its source in a God or many gods.

The dead really die. This bleak truth considered in isolation offers certain compensations to those who can face it squarely. Would we love so intensely if we knew there would never be any parting? What escape would there be from deepening melancholy, the growing weariness of more and more of the Same, if some conveyor belt carried us on and on for ever?

This is one side of a coin whose sharp contours cannot be softened by any top-dressing of sub-Christian sentimentality. But there is another side. The fact that Man dies proves that he is part of Nature; the fact that he fears death shows that he transcends Nature. He alone of all creatures (so far as we are aware) knows that there is a point in time when his existence will end. This fear of death is a complex thing; made up of a number of components. One is simple dread of the unknown. Another is a deeply-seated instinct that he deserves to die – this is the sting of death, a compound of guilt and anxiety. A third element in Man's attitude to death is an awareness that he is confronted by a mystery. I do not die like other creatures any more than I live like them. My reason cannot grasp what it means for a *me* to die. I am aware of what I stand to lose, but I can have no conception of what I might gain, or even who that *me* might be in a dimension totally beyond my comprehension.

At this point, the Christian Faith cuts like a lancet through the fog of speculation and conjecture. It firmly links death to sin, and has nothing whatever to say to those who deny either. The whole thrust of Biblical teaching is that Man has lost immortality because he has sinned – that is, separated himself from the Eternal. He is like a diver who chafes at the restriction of freedom caused by his air-line to the surface. So by cutting his air-pipe he gains greater freedom at the price of severing himself from the source of continued life. Death is the seal that attests Man's Declaration of Independence from God. Man chooses to be what God is. So be it. But he must derive the springs of his life from within himself. And because he shares the limitation of biological existence with the rest of Nature, so he dies. The immediate cause of death is certified with scientific detachment by some physician; its ultimate cause would make bizarre reading on any certificate, but is still true. Man dies because he plays at being God – and loses.

Nothing Man can do will alter this state of affairs because Creation itself is irreversible. Remember that Angel with the Flaming Sword which blocks the way back to the Garden of Eden? Yet even though Man is in a state of rebellion against God, he cannot merge completely into the natural world. He is still haunted by intimations of immortality. The anxiety, fear and mystery of death are symptomatic of the corruption of his original status as one made in the image of God, constructed as it were for perpetual union with the never-failing Source of all life.

We do well to pause here in order to make the point that this process of which sin is the cause and death the effect is not an individual transaction. My sinfulness is no private affair but an aspect of my solidarity with all mankind. Paul's epigram, 'The wages of sin is death', cannot be translated into the realm of scientific or historical fact, any more than a date can be put to the act of God's will by which nothingness became Creation. The totality of the truth about God, sin and death belongs to some super-history or inner-history which cannot be chronicled. That aspect of the reality of each as is accessible to the human mind only enters human history through the Christ-Event. A dim reflection of the character of God is seen in the life of Christ; the nature of sin is demonstrated in his Crucifixion and the answer to

147

the problem of death is proclaimed in the Resurrection.

Because Creation is irreversible, nothing and no one, not even God, can restore Man to primeval innocence. He must die, just as he is doomed to sin. But the Eternal becomes temporal in order that our eternity can be restored. Faith in Jesus is faith in his resurrection and implicit faith in our own resurrection. But just as the relationship between sin and death is not an individual transaction, so eternal life is more than a matter of individual survival. The dead really die. The light which Christianity sheds on the matter is to separate biological death from the death of the ego which occurs when by faith the Christian begins a new and risen life; part of the super-history that cannot be scientifically measured or naturally explained. To believe is to die the death that sin decrees, just as to believe is to rise again as a part of the New Humanity created beyond death by the resurrection of Jesus. Paul again – 'As in Adam all die, so in Christ shall all be made alive'. The Christian is someone whose death is already behind him in the ultimate sense. But this new life remains hidden in a mortal shell until death frees it.

To speculate what form eternal life takes when our natural death has been accomplished is a complete waste of time. We are historical beings, as little able to comprehend or even imagine what is beyond history as an ant would get the point of space flight by crawling across the plans of a moon rocket. How, then, can we know this unimaginable existence in a reality other than by its primary, glorious evidence in the Resurrection and Ascendancy of Jesus? The New Testament has an answer to that one which is deceptive in its simplicity – 'We know we have passed from death to life because we love the brethren'. Even Fred, for whom Eschatology is the name of a race horse, can understand that. Once we cease playing at God and receive his forgiveness, we become truly persons again. Creation has been re-

148

stored to its original order; those who believe live in, by and through God's love which is deathless. And because love is indivisible, we know that the Infinite has been joined to the finite, the Eternal to the temporal, not because we indulge in table-rapping or hear voices from the Beyond but because in down-to-earth, practical situations we give and receive love. All love requires some degree of self-transcendence and so strikes at the root of our egotism, which is the root of sin, the cause of our separation from God, the sting of death.

Nothing in the Bible gives us much of a clue as to where Fred is now or what form his personality takes. As Reinhold Niebhur has written, it behoves the Christian to maintain a resolute agnosticism about the furniture of heaven or the temperature of hell. The Christian affirms death but adds an all-important rider which is the basis of his hope – 'Whether we live or die, we are the Lord's'.

Just that. God on both sides of the void – the source of our regenerate life on this side of death and waiting to receive us on the other side.

Robert Herhold tells the story of an encounter between a member of his congregation who is a Chicago taxi-driver and a woman he picked up at a hospital. She broke into tears as the taxi drove away. After letting her cry for some time, the driver turned to her and said, 'It's none of my business, lady, but did something rough just happen back at the hospital?', 'Yes,' she replied, 'my mother just died.' The taxi-driver was silent for a while and then asked, 'Are you a Christian?' She said that she went to church regularly. 'What about your mother?' 'She was the best Christian I have ever known.' 'Then,' asked the taxi-driver, 'why are you crying as if everything was over?'[23]

Such home-spun wisdom is both a consolation and a warning. The Christian hope is of reunion within the New Humanity inaugurated by the resurrection of Jesus. The

149

grieving daughter and her dead mother already share the same life though the flux of Nature has severed physical contact. But the warning implicit in the assurance of reunion is of looking forward to death or even beyond it. This is not what the New Testament means by hope, but is the semi-pagan notion that our present life should be seen only as a preparation for death and eternity. The declaration that for the Christian he has his death already behind him, except in a biological sense, frees him from morbid speculation or other-worldly pietism so that he can concentrate all his efforts making *this* a good life. As Martin Luther King said, if there is no cause for which a man is prepared to put his life on the line then the stopping of his heart is merely a belated announcement of a death which has already taken place. Christian hope is just as much a political force as an eschatological reality. It liberates a man to struggle to provide the Old Humanity, which is still under God's providential care, with the conditions of justice, peace and joy to which it is entitled in a Creation that may be marred by Evil but still bears the marks of God's original intention and ultimate will.

To bring it all back to Fred. Christian hope is not only concerned with the meaning of his death but also with the problem of his unlived life. For the Christian, death is darkness filled with God. Unlived life is drabness filled with nothing.

Cry from the Tomb

If God had intended his 20th-century servants to have a stab at writing effective books commending the Christian Faith, he ought never to have created G. K. Chesterton. The man wrote like an angel and was as cunning as an old fox in his raids on the hen-runs of Atheism. He was, of course, a Catholic whilst I am a Protestant, and with due respect for the ecumenical spirit of our time, that is not a distinction to be belittled let alone ignored. He was also a man of his time. His popular works of Christian apologetics, *Orthodoxy* and *The Everlasting Man,* antedated by decades the Atom Bomb and the violent awakening of the Third World. There is a tinge of imperialistic red in his thinking and an unconscious assumption of the moral superiority of Western civilization that fiery radicals will certainly find jarring. His style is slightly redolent of the London club – well-worn leather, antique silver and hand-warmed port goblets. There is none of the clangour of a world in torment, wreaking of sweat, anger and blood.

And yet – to steep oneself in Chesterton's books is equally destructive of self-confidence and individuality of style. The pungent aphorisms, startling paradoxes and intricate arguments which sweep one along to some irresistible conclusion – Chesterton makes criminals of lesser writers. They soak up his style and become plagiarists against their will. Chesterton said it Better – those words are graven if not in letters of flame then burned with a hot poker into the surface of my desk.

This confession is necessary because I wish to challenge a hotpotch of misconceptions of Christianity against which Chesterton too directed a lethal pen. So I can't guarantee that he hasn't taken up residence like some benevolent genie in my typewriter. In spite of the generation gap and our widely divergent brands of churchmanship – I needn't even mention the obvious disparity in talent – we have common enemies. The difference is that whereas he devoured them whole, the best I can hope to do is yap at their heels and cause them some discomfort.

One plausible attack upon the integrity of Christianity is made by sophisticates who claim to be advocates of freedom of religious thought but are actually slaves to the dogmas of materialism. Obviously, I am not now concerned

151

with humanists or materialists who deny the existence of the supernatural. They can believe what they like; indeed, that's all they can believe – what they like. My target is the swinging theological iconoclast. I recognize one on sight, having been for years a member of the club. He will wriggle like Houdini to escape the chains of uncongenital theological dogmas without noticing that he's tied himself in knots which restrict his freedom in the opposite direction. The theological maverick reserves the right to believe what he likes about God but rejects God's right to believe what He likes about *him*. To take an obvious example. He demands the liberty to whittle down the number of Gospel miracles but denies God the liberty to perform more miracles. The right to doubt is an expression of Man's freedom but he will not swallow the idea that the right to perform miracles could be an expression of God's freedom too. He will approve of you as a liberal if you believe less than is customary about the Christian Faith but damn you as a fanatic if you believe more. He might even find it tolerably possible to accept that Jesus rose from the dead in some form or other but would snort with incredulity if you were to affirm that you expect your Aunt Lily to do the same.

Like the girl who announced that she was only slightly pregnant, the theological simplifier will accept that Christianity has a slightly supernatural element in it. To profess a full-blooded belief that Christianity is wholly supernatural in the sense that all its wholesome consequences are the result of God acting through obedient men is dismissed as a mental aberration. The effect of such theological antics on the laity is disastrous. There was a time when the man and woman in the pew felt obliged to hide the fact that they believed less Christian doctrine than their parson. Now some of them resort to subterfuge to keep from their parson the horrid truth that they believe more doctrine than he
152

does. They have it preached at them that pivotal points of Christianity such as the Incarnation, Resurrection and Ascension are myths, without having it brought to their attention that Man's myths could be God's truths – that such extraordinary events may be the only way that Divinity can communicate with Humanity in ways that are remotely understandable to the mind of Man.

Because Christianity is the historical result of the Eternal intersecting and penetrating the Natural, it will never be a series of neat logical propositions. It is a sprawling, untidy, even messy business where the limits of language are often reached and loose ends seem to dangle about all over the place. And every attempt made throughout Christian history to tidy up the mess by means of some complicated verbal formula generally raised more difficulties than it solved. But the fact that we are dealing with truths which do not fit neatly into words is not an argument for ditching the truths because our formulae are inadequate. The Athanasian Creed is a case in point. Its attempt to define the Trinity is a verbal quagmire. Some reductionists would turn us into Unitarians because the concept of one God *can* be expressed in words and is easier for the human mind to grasp. As they say, some of my best friends are Unitarians, and I admire their integrity, courage and single-minded search for the truth. But I am not a Unitarian, so I am forced to repeat the Athanasian Creed, though as infrequently as possible. And when I do, I add under my breath that its majestic, opaque phrases were the only words 5th-century scholars could find to express the odd truth that God is more like a Committee than a Monarch. Possibly the Trinitarian formula is a fancy way of saying that just as God gave Adam a companion because it is not good for Man to be alone, so he is revealing that it is not good for God to be alone either. The only true Man is Man-in-Community because the only true God is God-in-Community.

The motives of the simplifiers may be honourable, but their efforts in offering neat errors in place of untidy truths reduce Christianity to an ideology devoid of fire, poetry and mystery. And they are enemies of hope because they deny God's right to be himself, free to do whatever a good God chooses to do rather than operate within terms of reference laid down for him by some clever sceptic.

A current phenomenon which some desperate Christians hail as a sign of revival is that of the Jesus People. These young people are simplifiers *par excellence*. One must honour their rejection of the tawdry values of Western materialism and their desire to inject some joy into our tired, grey national life. But the most important thing about most of them is that they are idolators. Jesus is their present idol, just as ten years' ago it was Che Guevara and ten years from now it may be Joe or Josephine Bloggs. They want Jesus without Christianity and Christianity without the Church, and who can blame them? They wish to brush aside 20 centuries of Christian history and countless generations of the Jewish past and follow a Jesus without either forebears or posterity. And it isn't, alas, possible. Whoever chooses to follow Jesus has to conclude a package deal with history that includes Christianity, the Church and a whole lot of other things as well.

Sir Herbert Butterfield in the closing sentence of his *Christianity and History* unwittingly gave the Jesus People a motto when he wrote: 'Hold to Christ, and for the rest be totally uncommitted.' With all deference to a great historian, that isn't possible either. Would to God it were! The People of the Way have accumulated much luggage on their march through history, some of it the sheer dead-weight upon us of cruelty, intolerance and terror. There is blood on our hands and scars across our consciences. But not all our past has been sordid. God *has* spoken since the printers added the final full-stop to the Book of Revelation. We cannot disavow either the glory or the misery of our history. We are 20th-century Christians. That is the only breed extant.

The Jesus People are not the first movement in Christian history to weigh the Church in the balance and find it wanting. And we would be foolish to ignore the judgement upon us implied in their rejection of the institution and system of Christianity. But there is more to the Jesus-Event than a Galilean peasant who was a wandering story teller with nowhere to lay his head, exhibiting the joy and spontaneity which attracts the Jesus People to him. He was the key to a long and complex history – a Jew who inherited a blend of spiritual insight and political dynamus unique amongst all the peoples of the earth. He exercised a public ministry, died a public death as a result of confronting the power-groups of his day; he rose again from the dead to affirm a Lordship which his followers claimed was cosmic in scope. His proclamation of the Kingdom of God involves those who take him seriously in all the ambiguities of citizenship within two worlds. Jesus was not a private person and those who claim to follow him cannot contract out of the ongoing life of society as many of the Jesus People choose to do.

Far from lending itself to simplification, the Christian Faith is the most complex of all religions. To take just one unique element in it – Christianity adds two attributes to Divinity which are missing from other forms of Theism – courage and suffering. To create the world was an act of Divine courage; to forebear from blotting it out involves Divine suffering. Though it is technically incorrect to load down God with human attributes, our hope is vested not only in God's courage but also in his capacity to absorb suffering. That's a shortish sentence with implications it would take a life-time to think through.

The other great enemies of Christian hope are the ecclesi-

155

astical morticians who from their reading of history have not once but many times announced the final death of Christianity.[24] And the weight of history has been on their side. The Faith *has* died, even though its outer husk, the Church, has apparently still been thriving. Christianity has died many times – really and truly died, not merely sunk into a state of catalepsy like a sleeping princess awaiting the kiss of a lover who has fought his way through many perils to awaken her. The Christian Faith has died but rose again because it had a God who knew his way out of the grave.

Only the most naïve Christian would imagine that the Church and the Faith share the same history and fate like Siamese twins. There have been periods when the Church has been aglow with power and influence whilst beneath those magnificent vestments her heart has been dead and shrivelled. At other times, the Church has been laid waste, her building in ruins, her priests dead or in hiding, her status that of an official Enemy of the State – yet in upper rooms and dark cellars men and women have gathered in secret to pore over the Bible and break bread, proclaiming in a whisper the Lord's death till he come again.

It would take a potted history of Christianity, which I am not qualified to offer, to sketch out the dimensions of this strange truth. When the Roman Empire expired and the Dark Ages covered the earth, Church and State were so intertwined that it seemed inevitable that the Faith must die. Yet when the curtain rose on the next Act, the Middle Ages proper, there was Acquinas, occupying the chair Aristotle had vacated, surrounded by eager young men, prepared to live in tatters and exist on crusts in order to learn the new Faith, the resplendent reincarnation of an old one which had died. The mechanics of this extraordinary phenomenon only God knows. Just as Christ walked on water, so there have been times when the Christian Faith has walked on air as the foundations of her society crumbled under her and were swept away.

In North Africa, Islam put Christianity to the sword. In the Age of Reason bishops were agnostic about virtually everything except the quality of the wine in their cellars. When Darwin inaugurated the modern Age of Science by returning from the Galapagos Islands with a manuscript that appeared to incorporate Christianity's death certificate, for many men the Faith died. And now in the Age of Revolution when the Church seems irredeemably wedded to a Western society so reactionary that it must sooner or later be blown away by the great gusts of anger generated by the hungry and under-privileged of the world, the prospects of her survival are, to put it mildly, poor.

So the Faith has often died, and not always gloriously on a Cross but replete with old age and comfortably in its bed. Its doctrines have become so attenuated as to be as brittle as the bones of a senile pensioner; it has said its say and then its vocal chords have atrophied. But whether the mournful funeral procession has moved off from Golgotha or some musty death-chamber, men have seen the corpse laid to rest and gone away muttering 'And we thought that you might have saved Israel!'

Then has occurred a resurrection. God has found his way out of the tomb. This strange cycle makes the Christian Faith unique. When other religions die, they die for good and all. When Druidical religion passed away, it left behind only Stonehenge, and though there are still the faithful who once yearly enact the ritual of nostalgia by dancing round those monoliths, all their incantations cannot put fresh life into their gods. So too, many other religions have for a time taken possession of men's hearts and minds.

157

They had their day, and ceased to be. Christianity too, has, on many occasions, had its day and ceased to be. But it has risen spotless from the grave to take on a new lease of life.

I do not pretend to understand such things. Only God knows why death and resurrection is his chosen style of haunting history, and he is keeping that knowledge to himself. The fact that the death of Christianity is followed by resurrection is no cause for complacency amongst Christians. To live through the death of Faith is a terrifying, numbing thing.

So one must confess that those who with either a snort of derision or a sigh of regret pronounce the death of Christianity or of the Church or of both, may not be wrong. Possibly Christianity will die because it has been guilty of the unpardonable offence of boring people – like the senile old man who tells long-winded stories, full of reminiscence, to any he can persuade to listen to him. Possibly the day may not be far off when tourists throng Westminster Abbey or St Paul's Cathedral or St Peter's, Rome, as they throng Stonehenge to visit the crumbling artifacts of a dead Faith. The boring old man has died in his bed. Really died, because there comes a point in the dissolution of an organism when change is irreversible – neither the Kiss of Life nor all the gleaming equipment of the Intensive Care Unit is of any avail.

What then? What now? Christian hope is in no way related to membership statistics or churchgoing habits. It takes seriously the possibility that the defiant cries of optimism of those who detect a diamond in the glitter of light from a worthless piece of glass serve only to drown the death-rattle of the Christian Faith. Christian hope is not based upon the signs of the times, for they are unpropitious, nor on any sub-Christian utopianism which cannot conceive of the death of Faith. Instead, it listens carefully for
158

the cry from the tomb as the God who is adept at finding his way out of the grave rises to offer new life through a Faith that has undergone the full rigour of its death.

That is not a firm diagnosis; just the offer of a suggestion. When the going gets rough and the Christian must live through that eternity between Crucifixion and Resurrection which the saints called the Dark Night of the Soul, he should stop his ears to the soothsayers of easy optimism or prognosticators of doom and listen instead for subterranean thunder – the echo of God's Word, which according to Jeremiah, is a hammer that splinters rock.

Notes

1. *Include Me Out* (Epworth, 1968). *Unyoung, Uncoloured, Unpoor* (Epworth, 1968).
2. Quoted in: Gardner, *Self-Renewal* (Harper, 1965), p. 122.
3. Ibid., p. 111.
4. See pp. 17–18 of my *Mankind my Church* (Hodder, 1971).
5. Russell, *Autobiography* (Allen and Unwin, 1967), Vol. 1, p. 13.
6. Ibid.
7. Adapted from title of book by Denis Gabor (Penguin, 1963).
8. I Cor. 1. 28 (N.E.B.).
9. Knox, *Limits of Unbelief* (Collins, 1970).
10. See: Pelz, *True Deceivers* (Collins, 1966), p. 100 *et seq.*
11. Furlong, *Travelling In* (Hodder and Stoughton, 1971).
12. Gabor, *Inventing the Future* (Penguin, 1963), p. 130.
13. Quoted from: 'What Keeps a Businessman Busy'– Lecture given at University of St Andrews by Andrew M. Knox.
14. Adapted from *Can Man Care for the Earth?* Ed. Heiss and McInnis (Abingdon, 1971).
15. Title of book, Hodder and Stoughton, 1971.
16. Chesterton, *The Everlasting Man* (Hodder and Stoughton, 1928).
17. See: Trueblood, *The Humour of Christ* (Harper, 1964).
18. Niebuhr, *Beyond Tragedy* (Scribner, 1937), p. 27 *et seq.*
19. Marty, *The Search for a Usable Future* (Harper, 1969), ch. 9.
20. Pelz, *True Deceivers* (Collins, 1966), p. 55.
21. See: Lewis, *Miracles* (Bles, 1947).
22. Quoted by Cowen, *The Foundations of Freedom* (Oxford, 1961), p. 195.
23. Herhold, *Funny, You Don't Look Christian* (Weybright, 1969), p. 66.
24. Chesterton, *The Everlasting Man* (Hodder and Stoughton, 1928), ch. 6.